The AFRICANS
Study Guide

This book was developed for general use as the study guide for a telecourse. *The Africans* telecourse consists of nine one-hour public television programs, a text, a study guide, and a faculty guide. The series was produced by WETA-TV, Washington, D.C., and the BBC with major funding provided by The Annenberg/CPB Project. Additional funding comes from the National Endowment for the Humanities, the Public Broadcasting Service, and the Corporation for Public Broadcasting. Project director and executive producer of *The Africans* is Charles Hobson, Senior Vice President – Special Projects, WETA-TV.

For further information on telecourse licensing, purchase of pre-recorded video-cassettes, and print materials, contact:

 The Annenberg/CPB Collection

1213 Wilmette Avenue
Wilmette, IL 60091
1-800 LEARNER (532-7637)
(In Illinois 312-256-3200)

The AFRICANS
Study Guide

Managing Editor
Toby Kleban Levine

Contributing Editor
Colin M. Turnbull

Coordinating Editors
Tracy Burke Carrier
Frieda Lindfield Werden

PRAEGER

New York
Westport, Connecticut
London

Library of Congress Cataloging in Publication Data

Main entry under title:

The Africans : a reader.

Text developed as a companion volume to the public
television series, The Africans, co-produced by the
British Broadcasting Corporation and WETA/TV,
Washington, D.C.
  Includes bibliographies and index.
  1. Africa-Civilization. I. Mazrui, Ali Al'Amin.
II. Levine, Toby Kleban. III. Africans (Television
program)
DT14.A3745 1986   960   85-28166

Cover Illustration by Mark English

Library of Congress Catalog Card Number: 85-28166
ISBN: 0-275-92074-7

First published in 1986

Praeger Publishers, One Madison Avenue, New York, NY 10010
An imprint of Greenwood Publishing Group, Inc.

Printed in the United States of America

The paper used in this book complies with the Permanent
Paper Standard issued by the National Information Standards
Organization (Z39.48-1984).

10 9 8 7 6

Table of Contents

Introducing *The Africans*

The Africans, a major new prime-time public television series and telecourse premiering in the fall of 1986, is a view of Africa from the inside looking out. At its core is the thesis that contemporary Africa is a product of three major influences – an indigenous heritage, Western culture, and Islamic culture. The coexistence of these three legacies helps to explain the diversity of the continent and the people who are called African. To understand and illustrate this diversity, members of the project have gone to nearly 20 African countries and have consulted with scholars throughout the world.

The Africans looks at examples of both cultural conflict and cultural synthesis. It shows the impact of geography on African history as well as the variety of environments and lifestyles within contemporary Africa. It explores the coexistence and interlocking influences of the three religious heritages and the means by which Africa's human and natural resources have been exploited. It examines Africa's experiments with different forms of government and assesses the problems of a continent that is caught between dependency and decay. Finally, the course considers Africa in the context of its relations with the rest of the world.

The Africans is a co-production of WETA-TV, the public television station in Washington, D.C., and the British Broadcasting Corporation.

Major funding for *The Africans* is provided by The Annenberg/CPB Project. Additional funding is from the National Endowment for the Humanities, the Public Broadcasting Service, and the Corporation for Public Broadcasting.

The Africans is closed captioned for the hearing impaired.

Series Host

Ali A. Mazrui, host of *The Africans*, is professor of political science at the University of Michigan and research professor at the University of Jos, Nigeria. In *The Africans*, Mazrui presents the Africa of his experience, drawing on the knowledge of scholars throughout the world. Mazrui, a native Kenyan, earned a B.A. from Manchester University, an M.A. from Columbia University, and a doctorate from Oxford University. He taught at Makerere University in Uganda for ten years and is an editor of UNESCO's projected eight-volume history of Africa. He also has served as president of the African Studies Association in the United States and as host of "Searching for a New Zimbabwe," a BBC *Panorama* production. In 1979, he delivered the BBC Reith Lectures entitled *The African Condition*.

The *Africans* Design Team

ADVISORY COMMITTEE

Mbye Cham
African Studies and Research Program
Howard University

Christopher Davis-Roberts
Center for Afro-American and African Studies and
Department of Anthropology
University of Michigan

Jacques Dubois
Special Academic Areas
Prince George's Community College (Maryland)

Joseph E. Harris
Department of History
Howard University

Fred M. Hayward
Department of Political Science
University of Wisconsin/ Madison

Victor T. Le Vine
Department of Political Science
Washington University/St. Louis

Merrick Posnansky
Departments of History and Anthropology and
Institute of Archaeology
University of California/Los Angeles

Pearl T. Robinson
Department of Political Science
Tufts University

Robert I. Rotberg
Departments of Political Science and History
Massachusetts Institute of Technology

Elliott P. Skinner
Department of Anthropology
Columbia University

Colin M. Turnbull
Research Associate
The American Museum of Natural History

PRODUCTION

Charles Hobson, American project director and executive producer, is senior vice president of special projects at WETA-TV. Hobson has been project director/executive producer of numerous educational and public television projects, including the 13-part telecourse *From Jumpstreet: A Story of Black Music*.

David Harrison, British project director and executive producer, formerly was deputy editor of the BBC's *Panorama* series. Harrison received the British Royal Television Society's Supreme Award for the best documentary of 1979 and has been filming in Africa for 12 years.

Peter Bate, producer, has filmed in 20 countries in the past ten years, specializing in Middle East issues. Prior to his work on *The Africans*, he produced *Hanging Fire*, a four-part series on Israel; edited film for the BBC; and was a producer of the BBC's *Panorama* series.

Tim Copestake, producer, specializes in the production of current affairs programs at the BBC. He is a graduate of Oxford University and the London International Film School and was film editor of an EMMY-award-winning program for *Panorama* about Georgi Markov and arms trade in South Africa.

Diana Frank, senior researcher, is research coordinator for special projects at WETA-TV. She is a graduate of Georgetown University (Phi Beta Kappa) and earned a Ph.D. in linguistics from Cornell University. She also is the author of a novel in Danish, *Et Uaar*.

TELECOURSE DESIGN

Toby Kleban Levine, telecourse director and print managing editor, is president of Toby Levine Communications. She formerly was director of educational activities at WETA-TV where she served as curriculum director of *From Jumpstreet* and project manager of *Congress: We The People*, in addition to managing a telecourse programming service for local colleges.

Tracy Burke Carrier, print coordinating editor, came to the project from Cairo, where she taught English to Egyptians. She also has been an editor and broadcast specialist at Virginia Commonwealth University and an announcer and community affairs director at WRFK-FM, the public radio station in Richmond.

Frieda Lindfield Werden, editorial consultant, is a writer and editor whose experience includes scholarly presses, trade press, and textbook publishing. Recently, she served as series producer for National Public Radio's *Faces, Mirrors, Masks: 20th Century Latin American Fiction,* 13 half-hour sound portraits of writers and their culture.

Special thanks to Ellen Casey, Carol Gasparach, Vernetta Gill, Caren Levine, Judith Pickford-Barse, Steven Reichert, and Emily Stuman.

The Telecourse

The Africans telecourse consists of 13 weeks of study. The first two weeks of course study, to be completed prior to the start of the broadcast of the television programs, will introduce you to the major concepts of the course and particularly to the concepts that underlie the indigenous aspects of Africa's heritage. Beginning with the third week of the course, reading and print study assignments correlate directly to the nine programs in the television series. The final two weeks of assignments are designed to be completed after broadcast of the series has concluded.

By the completion of the course, you should

- understand the diversity of Africa, the range of successes and failures that have occurred there, and Africa's relationship to other parts of the world;
- be able to discuss Africa's past and present as a means of understanding its future, illustrating themes from both individual and societal points of view;
- have developed tools for analyzing social change in Africa; and
- be able to illustrate adaptation and readaptation within the global context.

TELEVISION PROGRAMS

The Africans consists of nine one-hour programs.

Anatomy of a Continent examines Africa as the birthplace of humankind and discusses the impact of geography on African history, including the role of the Nile in the origin of civilization and the introduction of Islam to Africa through its Arabic borders.

The Triple Heritage of Lifestyles explores how African contemporary lifestyles are influenced by indigenous, Western, and Islamic factors and questions whether Westernization is reversible. The program compares simple African societies with those that are more complex and centralized and focuses on the importance of family life.

New Gods examines the factors that influence religion in Africa, paying particular attention to how traditional African religions, Islam, and

Christianity coexist and influence each other. It also explores the extent to which Christianity and Islam are becoming Africanized.

Exploitation contrasts the impact of the West on Africa and the impact of Africa on the development of the West, looking at the manner in which Africa's human and natural resources have been exploited before, during, and after the colonial period.

New Conflicts explores the tensions inherent in the juxtaposition of the three heritages, looking at the ways in which these conflicts have contributed to the rise of the nationalist movement, the warrior tradition of indigenous Africa, the *jihad* (holy war) tradition of Islam, and modern guerilla warfare.

In Search of Stability studies several means of governing. New social orders are examined to illustrate an Africa in search of a viable form of government in the post-independence period. The program asks which efforts have succeeded, which have failed, and why.

A Garden of Eden in Decay? identifies the problems of a continent that produces what it does not consume and consumes what it does not produce, showing Africa's struggle between economic dependency and decay.

A Conflict of Cultures shows the coexistence of many African traditions and modern activities and the conflicts and compromises which emerge from the mixing of cultures. It explores whether Africa can synthesize its own heritage with the legacies of Islam and the West.

Africa in the World illustrates African contributions to contemporary culture, including the significance of the African diaspora, particularly in North America, and examines the continuing influence of the superpowers on the affairs of the continent.

RELATED READING

Two major books have been developed to assist your study of *The Africans*. Please check with your faculty to determine which books are assigned for this course.

The Africans: A Reader, edited by Ali A. Mazrui and Toby Kleban Levine (New York: Praeger Publishers, 1986), was prepared to serve as the telecourse text. Twelve scholars worked together to present the major concepts of the course and to introduce a variety of historical and contemporary writings on Africa. Each section of the book consists of an essay by the chapter coordinator and a selection of extracts from primary sources. Among the authors whose work is included are Chinua Achebe; Adebayo Adedeji; Georges Balandier; Heinrich Barth; Ibn Battuta; John Miller Chernoff; J. Sorie Conteh; Francis Mading Deng; Buchi Emecheta; E. E. Evans-Pritchard; Alexander Falconbridge; Marcus Garvey; André Gide; Marcel Griaule; Carol Hermer; Jacques Louis Hymans; Ryszard Kapuscinski; Jomo Kenyatta; Colin Legum; Godfrey Lienhardt; Alain Locke; Nelson Mandela; Judith Miller; Erasto Muga; George S. Mwase; Abioseh Nicol; Kwame Nkrumah; Gabriel Okara; Francis Ernest Kobina Parkes; Audrey Richards; Pearl T. Robinson; Jacques Roumain; Marjorie Shostak; Wole Soyinka; Victor Turner; Desmond Tutu; Ngugi wa Thiong'o; Dunstan M. Wai; and Freda Wolfson.

The Africans: A Triple Heritage by Ali A. Mazrui (New York: Little, Brown and Company, 1986) offers a challenging view of Africa and presents an expanded view of the themes Mazrui introduces in the television programs. Among the topics Mazrui addresses are: the ancient and new triple heritages of Africa; a definition of Africa according to race, continent, and power; Africans' ability to adapt to harsh environmental conditions; the entry of Christianity and Islam into Africa; the effect of religion on culture and politics; states and stateless societies; and the problems of economic dependency and development.

TAKING *THE AFRICANS* AS A TELECOURSE

There is no right or wrong way to approach *The Africans* telecourse. There are, however, a number of suggestions that can be made that have worked for other telecourse students.

1. As soon after registration as possible, find out the following:

- what books are required for the course
- if and when an orientation session has been scheduled
- when *The Africans* will be broadcast in your area (If there is more than one public television station there may be several opportunities for you to watch the programs. Further, many public television stations will repeat the program at least once during the week it is first shown. Determine at what time you will watch it and make this an inviolate part of your schedule. Remember there are no viewing assignments during the first two weeks and last two weeks of the course.)

- when examinations are scheduled for the course (Put these in your calendar.)
- if any additional on-campus meetings have been scheduled (Make plans to attend as many review sessions, seminars, etc., as possible.)

2. Although the print materials may be read in any order, given a choice, read the Study Guide chapter first, at least through the unit section called "Study Focus Questions." This will give you an overview of the week's work and suggest some unifying themes that you can be thinking about as you view the associated programs and read the text.

3. When you read the assigned text chapters, read the entire chapter, including the readings. These are a fundamental part of the course and will give the most specific and personal views of different African societies and their responses to the triple heritage.

4. Some students have found that notetaking while viewing the television programs is helpful; others find it distracting and find it helpful to audiotape the program for later review. It is permissible to videotape the programs *for your own personal review only*. It will probably be helpful for you to view the programs twice whenever possible.

5. After you have viewed the program and read the related text chapter, it probably will be helpful to return to the Study Guide to consider the listing of Key Words and Concepts and the Questions for Review. This will help prepare you both for specific, short-answer-type questions on examinations and for more wide-ranging short essay questions. In some cases, the Questions for Review require that you think about the content of the unit in a context beyond that specifically presented by the reading or program. They will require you to think about the application of what you have learned to the future of Africa.

6. Keep up with course assignments on a weekly basis. Some students have found that entering study activities in a study log helps them to focus on what assignments require their attention. This is also a good place to note questions for the course instructor and to judge the best order of study and review for you.

7. Keep in touch with your instructor. Know when he or she has call-hours and how to reach him or her by mail. The instructor would like to hear from you and to know how you are doing in the course. You do not need to wait until you have a problem. Call to discuss the content of the course and to obtain clarification of course content.

8. Given the content of this course, it is absolutely essential that you read the newspaper daily. During the period of time this course was being produced there were numerous changes taking place in Africa on a daily basis. In fact, to be able to produce programs that were as current as possible, the final editing of the television programs was completed fairly close to when the programs were first broadcast. Publication needs required that the text and study guide be completed somewhat earlier. There may be discrepancies between the two, therefore, as indeed there may be differences between the program and the current situation in Africa at the time you take the course.

WEEK 1

Indigenous Africa

OBJECTIVES

After reading this week's assignments you should be able to:

- Identify the cultures included in the triple heritage;
- Discuss the roles of witchcraft and divination in an indigenous African culture;
- Describe and compare at least two rituals that are used in indigenous African cultures to mark the passage of youth into adulthood.

STUDY RESOURCES

Check with your instructor for specific assignments.

Television Program
    There is no viewing assignment this week.
The Africans: A Reader
    Preface
    Part I, "Indigenous Africa" through Reading I.6
    by Christopher Davis-Roberts
The Africans: A Triple Heritage by Ali A. Mazrui
    Introduction: "A Celebration of Decay"

STUDY FOCUS by Colin M. Turnbull

Throughout this series a central theme is Africa's triple heritage: the interaction of indigenous African, Western, and Islamic cultures. In this first chapter, we begin by focusing on indigenous Africa, the Africa that forms the bedrock of the triple heritage. It has accepted the other religions and ways of life, adapted them to its needs, and made them its own.

There are several vital issues that should be faced squarely in any attempt to understand "Africa" or "Africans." The first question is, Can we reasonably generalize about the whole of Africa? On the whole, the answer to that is yes. In spite of the enormous diversity of outward form there is a high degree of fundamental similarity among indigenous African cultures. Among the many common elements may be found: the importance of cooperation and harmonious community interactions (as contrasted with the rampant individuality of Western culture); the ability to adapt readily to new circumstances, and to assimilate new elements without losing their own fundamental character; the virtually sacred status of family and the land; a sense of unity with the rest of nature, and a belief that the vital force which permeates all things can be manipulated for either good or ill; a belief in the continuous participation of ancestors and the dead in the life of the community; the use of divination to determine the relationship between good or bad behavior and other events, particularly deaths and illnesses; the concept of witchcraft as an explanation for specific events; and an aesthetic approach to all of daily life.

The first reading accompanying Professor Davis-Roberts' essay shows how intimately the African aesthetic relates to social life. It indicates that the very structure of musical form may relate directly to vitally important social values. For instance, in African music many rhythms may come together, each responding to the others without losing its own individuality, but subtly adapting it so that it adds to the others. Combined, the result is something much greater than any one rhythm on its own. This creates a precise musical model for the ideal relationship that in African society should exist between individuals, all of whom should be willing to modify their behavior so as to create a harmonious community. Other art forms tell a similar story. Any consideration of aesthetics is inseparable from a consideration of ethics, of questions of character, or of what kinds of human behavior are good or bad. Aesthetics also demand a consideration of almost all other aspects of social life: domestic, economic, political, and certainly religious. Here in a land of immense diversity, the first lesson we have to learn is one of unity, cohesion, and human concern.

Another question we must ask is, How can we interpret events so as to arrive at a genuine understanding of Africa and the Africans? Our own lifelong experience limits our understanding, creating a natural tendency to ethnocentrism that is not easy to break even when we are conscious of it. But failure to escape the confines of our own culture dooms any attempt to understand another culture. For instance, it is all too easy to be misled by such comfortably familiar words as *family*. But the African's concept of family is much bigger than a Westerner's, including, for instance, the children of his siblings. In our highly mobile world, it is difficult to keep in touch with even the closest members of our families; and loss of a family member is primarily a personal and social tragedy. But in Africa, if a family member is taken away – to go to school in the city, for instance – the loss is also economic, political, and spiritual, for the family is security and the promise of the future. More than merely a biological group, the family is a complete cooperative. In addition to family ties, Africans recognize other social bonding mechanisms, including ties related to age, gender, and territory. Initiation and other rites of passage are important in defining and clarifying these ties and the responsibilities they engender.

We have to be even more wary of ethnocentrism when it comes to practices that seem strange to us. While at one level Africans treat the world of nature as "natural" in the Western sense of the word, at another level, because of its inherent order, nature is invested with symbolic meaning and becomes truly supernatural. What in the old days Westerners took to be superstition and ignorance, seen in this light proves to be a highly sophisticated philosophy. Like their aesthetics, the Africans' use of divination and belief in witchcraft reflects a central concern with order, and particularly with the healthy, ordered relationships that should ideally exist between all human beings. At this opening stage of the course, we have to come to grips with the problem of translation, not just of language, but of thoughts and actions, and here we are given the opportunity to begin.

This week's readings introduce several features of indigenous African experience in order to establish an understanding of the culture that existed prior to the integration and juxtaposition of Islamic and Western culture. Among the concepts introduced through the readings are the role of music and movement, witchcraft, and divination. Several initiation rites also are described.

Primary source readings include selections from the following: John Miller Chernoff, *African Rhythm and African Sensibility* ; Edward Evans Evans-Pritchard, *Witchcraft, Oracles, and Magic Among the Azande*; Victor Turner, *Revelation and Divination in Ndembu Ritual*; Victor Turner, *The Forest of Symbols*; Jomo Kenyatta, *Facing Mount Kenya*; and Audrey I. Richards, *Chisungu: A Girls' Initiation Ceremony Among the Bemba of Zambia.*

STUDY FOCUS QUESTIONS

- What basic values of African culture can be observed in each of the readings following Professor Davis-Roberts' essay?
- How would witchcraft and divination be viewed from an ethnocentric Western perspective? How might they be viewed from an indigenous African perspective? What elements in Western culture serve similar functions?
- Why is initiation a matter of lifelong importance in indigenous societies?

KEY WORDS AND CONCEPTS

causation
circumcision
clitoridectomy
divination
indigenous
initiation
interdependence
polymetric rhythms
productive sector
sacrifice
symbols
triple heritage

QUESTIONS FOR REVIEW

1. What are romantic gloriana and romantic primitivism? How might these concepts be related to ethnocentrism?

2. Compare and contrast the indigenous, Islamic, and Western Christian views on the relationship of humans and nature, what is considered sacred and profane, and the roles and rights of women.

3. What qualities do the Ndembu consider good ones for a person to have, and what qualities are considered bad? Are these same qualities

good and bad in Western culture, too, or are other values considered more important?

4. What rights and roles do women have among the Bemba? What conflicts can be seen in women's lives? Are any of them resolved as the women grow older?

ADDITIONAL RECOMMENDED READINGS

Chernoff, John Miller. *African Rhythm and African Sensibility*. Chicago: University of Chicago Press, 1981.

Evans-Pritchard, Edward Evans. *Witchcraft, Oracles, and Magic Among the Azande*. New York: Oxford at the Clarendon Press, 1937.

Kenyatta, Jomo. *Facing Mount Kenya: The Tribal Life of the Gikuyu*. New York: Vintage Books, 1962.

Richards, Audrey. *Chisungu: A Girls' Initiation Ceremony Among the Bemba of Zambia*. New York: Tavistock Publications, 1982.

Turner, Victor. *The Forest of Symbols: Aspects of Ndembu Ritual*. Ithaca: Cornell University Press, 1967.

Turner, Victor. *Revelation and Divination in Ndembu Ritual*. Ithaca: Cornell University Press, 1975.

WEEK 2

Indigenous Africa, Continued

OBJECTIVES

After reading this week's assignments you should be able to:

- Cite specific examples of ways aesthetics permeate all of African life;
- Give examples of the importance Africans place on *how* an activity is carried out and discuss why method is often more important than result;
- Discuss aspects of the relationships between the dead and the living in indigenous culture;
- Describe several methods of healing used in indigenous Africa.

STUDY RESOURCES

Check with your instructor for specific assignments.

Television Program
There is no viewing assignment this week.
The Africans: A Reader
Part I, "Indigenous Africa," Readings I.7-I.11
selected and introduced
by Christopher Davis-Roberts
The Africans: A Triple Heritage by Ali A. Mazrui
Chapter 3, "The Indigenous Personality"

STUDY FOCUS by Colin M. Turnbull

The primary focus this week is still on what can be referred to as indigenous Africa. The question of what is indigenous in Africa today is not an easy one to answer. Contemporary Africa is what it is because of a multitude of factors and a multitude of foreign influences, ranging far beyond the dominant ones of Christianity and Islam. Archeological work has uncovered proof of ancient Chinese influence, for instance; and the existence of certain forms of vegetation demonstrates contact with South America. So it is with any known culture: we are all the product of many influences. There is no such thing as a "pure" culture, if by that we mean one untainted with the outside world.

Today, Africa is being bombarded by external influences, ranging from economic aid through political alignments and missionary endeavors to the considerable cultural impact of tourism. These influences are primarily European and Arab (and increasingly American), Christian and Muslim (and increasingly agnostic, if not atheistic). The cultural scene is every bit as volatile, if not more so, than the economic or political scene. Nevertheless, it is important to try to isolate the various elements of African culture, and for more reasons than mere historical curiosity. The question of origins rouses powerful emotions, and that in itself is a major political factor and can easily become an economic factor as well. Perhaps we are in quest of a myth when we look for the indigenous culture of Africa; but the myth itself has a reality of its own. The rigorous pursuit of it is an exciting journey that reveals much about *all* the various components of that which is truly African today.

In our search for what is truly African, we may first wish to turn to archeology. From human remains, archeologists have learned something about what the very first Africans looked like; and from the study of these ancients' physiology they can better understand the lifestyles revealed by excavations of early hunting sites and cave dwellings. A continuity can be traced from these early sites to the ancient cities that once were spread throughout the continent. From the archeologists, we can learn something about the economic life of these early Africans, something of their political organization and religious life, and a great deal about their domestic organization. But that is all remote; and while some continuity can be traced through to the present day, that is a hazardous journey. The "basic African" today may be as different from the ancients in culture as in physique.

Another way of looking for a "pure" Africa, relatively untouched by foreign influences, might be to turn to groups of contemporary hunter-gatherers such as the Hadza of Tanzania, the San of the Kalahari, and the Mbuti of the rain forest. These peoples still live much as early Africans lived. They need and use an absolute minimum of foreign technology, and even have little or no need for metal, though some may use it. Their ancient ancestry and isolation – and so, "purity" – can be supported genetically. Such populations are immensely useful to us in thinking about "the basic African," because in their cultures – which are by no means as simple as they are sometimes imagined to be – we find dominant, distinctive cultural traits that are also clearly seen in more apparently Westernized, complex, contemporary African society. The peoples themselves, however, cannot be called "basic Africans," for the good and curiously African reason that each is so specifically adapted to its own environment – the grasslands, the desert, or the rain forest.

Another way of seeking out what is basically African is to eliminate that which is plainly due to external influence. For example, in one nominally Christian African village the communion wine is poured on the ground rather than put to the lips of the communicant. Two rites are at work here: the serving of the wine is clearly Christian, and the pouring of the wine on the ground is clearly something else. In the latter we recognize the desire to incorporate the ancestors into what is going on in the contemporary world. We also get some idea as to the true "Africanity" of whatever trait we are looking at by seeing how widespread it is – and indeed we find reverence for the ancestors to be spread throughout the entire continent, if manifest in many different ways.

Yet another test of the Africanity of a cultural trait is to see how well it fits in with, and becomes an integral part of, the physical environment. Of course, given massive movements of populations many traits that originated in one environment, such as the grasslands, may be transported into a totally different environment, such as the tropical rain forest. But wherever Africans find themselves, they seem to make a strongly religious connection with the environment. It would be very un-African if they were to practice Christianity exactly as it is practiced in Europe or America, performing the same rituals in the same way.

This week's reading assignment brings us back, through a consideration of storytelling and poetry, to some of the basic lessons constantly reiterated by the structure and form of African aesthetics. Examples are given that deal with the relation of society to the individual, the relationship of parents to children, and of rulers to ruled. We see that an ancient aesthetic and religious tradition is as alive and as vital today as it ever was, and is continuing its work in helping them to retain their own individualities, their own identities, while seeing themselves as an equal and vital part of something much bigger. In the excerpts Professor Davis-Roberts provides, it can be seen that indigenous Africans express their creativity in many realms, among them: philosophy and theology; linguistic expressions of purely aesthetic concepts; poetry in the form of songs and hymns; and also writing in Western genres – in this case, the modern novel. In addition, the African aesthetic can be seen to be operative in personal relations, acting to temper the grosser human motives such as power or gain. By no means the least lesson to learn from this chapter is that the Africans are concerned with human relationships that are not merely orderly and effective, but that are also filled with beauty, caring, and human concerns.

Primary source readings for this week are excerpted from: Marcel Griaule, *Conversations with Ogotemmêli: An Introduction to Dogon Religious Ideas*; Godfrey Lienhardt, *Divinity and Experience: The Religion of the Dinka*; Paul Riesman, *Freedom in Fulani Social Life: An Introspective Ethnography*; and Buchi Emecheta, *The Joys of Motherhood*.

STUDY FOCUS QUESTIONS

As you complete this week's assignment, consider the following questions.

- What are some of the social "functions" of African aesthetics, and can comparable functions be found in our society?
- What areas of freedom of choice do you find built into the structures of the traditional societies described?
- In last week's readings, we gained some insight into the indigenous view that incorrect behavior can cause illnesses and other events. What relations of causality can be seen in this week's readings between individuals' actions and things that happen to themselves and others?

KEY CONCEPTS AND NAMES

ancestors
complete woman
creativity
freedom
money economy
obedience
polygyny

quality of life
respect
self-control
shame

QUESTIONS FOR REVIEW

1. How does Ogotemmêli define the Word? Can this conversation be compared to anything in Western experience?

2. What are the relationships between the concepts of freedom and obedience in Fulani terms? Between work and freedom?

3. How does traditional Ibo culture fit into the plot of Emecheta's novel? How does culture shape Agbadi's and Ona's characters and their relationship?

4. What universal human characteristics are revealed in a comparison between the indigenous African cultures described in the chapter readings and our own?

ADDITIONAL RECOMMENDED READINGS

Emecheta, Buchi. *The Joys of Motherhood.* New York: George Braziller, Inc., 1979.

Griaule, Marcel. *Conversations with Ogotemmêli: An Introduction to Dogon Religious Ideas.* New York: Oxford at the Clarendon Press, 1961.

Lienhardt, Godfrey. *Divinity and Experience: The Religion of the Dinka.* New York: Oxford at the Clarendon Press, 1961.

Riesman, Paul. *Freedom in Fulani Social Life: An Introspective Ethnography.* Chicago: University of Chicago Press, 1977.

WEEK 3

The Anatomy of a Continent

OBJECTIVES

After reading this week's assignments and viewing the related television program, you should be able to:

- Name the major geographic features of Africa;
- Discuss how African geography and climate facilitate or constrain migration and settlement;
- Describe the geographic and environmental relationship of Africa to the Arabian peninsula and identify results of that relationship;
- Discuss the adaptation to their environments made by a hunting and gathering society, a pastoralist society, and a nomadic society.

STUDY RESOURCES

Check with your instructor for specific assignments.

Television Program
1. "Anatomy of a Continent"
The Africans: A Reader
Chapter 1, "Anatomy of a Continent"
by Merrick Posnansky
The Africans: A Triple Heritage by Ali A. Mazrui
Chapter 1, "Where Is Africa?"
Chapter 2, "Anatomy of a Continent"

TELEVISION PROGRAM

This program examines perhaps the most powerful indigenous forces of all – Africa's geography and climate – and focuses on the effect of water, wind, and time. The ability of people to overcome these elements and to form a strong viable culture is shown in Egypt, the birthplace of the Pharaonic dynasties three thousand years before Christ. The program also looks at the impact of geography on African culture, examining the Arabic borders across which Islam was introduced to indigenous Africa.

STUDY FOCUS by Colin M. Turnbull

No single factor is more crucial to our understanding of Africa than the environment. The vast size of the continent is matched by the diversity that characterizes it, a diversity that is directly related to the richness of the peoples and their cultures. A consideration of the African environment is as vital for our understanding of the Africa of the past as it is for our understanding of Africa today.

The environmental factor is just as essential to an understanding of Africa in relation to the rest of the world. It helps to explain the nature of foreign influence and intervention, the spread of foreign religions through the continent, the coming of economic and political exploitation in the forms of slavery and colonialism, and the continued presence of foreign peoples and foreign influence in many newly independent nations. It also suggests why the whole of the enormously rich southern part of Africa is still under a foreign domination that shows no signs of granting to its African majority any true measure of participation in their own government.

This week's program and readings explore the intimate relationship between the land and the people. Deserts and tropical rain forests, a coastline with few natural harbors (except in the far north and far south), a hot, humid climate, icy mountain ranges, and low lying rivers that breed some of the more lethal sources of sickness and disease in the world all have profoundly influenced population movement and settlement. Particularly affected were the European immigrants who did not have the Africans' natural resistance to many of these diseases. Geographical features also have helped shape political boundaries, not so much because they were barriers to movement or impossible to settle, but because each distinctive environment gave rise to an equally distinctive and enduring cultural adaptation. This adaptability of the African peoples is one of the many characteristics that they share despite their diversity. Closely linked to it is the intimacy of their shared relationship with the natural world around them. Even in the modern cities and shanty town slums of industrial Africa, a relationship to the land remains sacred to life and thought.

In tracing the history of the continent with its periodic and sometimes disastrous climatic changes, a parallel history of ongoing human ingenuity and inventiveness emerges. Social systems geared to one environmental context are constantly adapting to meet the changing face of the land. Compare this to other forms of change, such as adaptation to foreign influence, new technologies, new political systems, and new religious beliefs. In fact, the obvious resilience of traditional African cultures and their genius for survival should make us question whether tradition is indeed as hostile to modernization and nationalism as had been supposed. Contemporary governments are discovering that some of their more precious resources lie in ancient traditions that have taught all Africans not only how to adapt technologically to the demands of their environment, but also how to build new unities that are still firmly rooted in the land.

Professor Posnansky's chapter explores the general features of Africa which gave it its distinctive geographic personality and the ways in which different communities have adapted to their environments. He discusses the impact of climatic changes on African history, the relationship of vegetation and soils to the geography of the continent, and patterns of disease that have plagued the continent. In order to understand the environmental adaptations made by populations in Africa, primary source readings introduce Africans who engage in various methods to obtain their daily food. Historical insight and a discussion of the importance of the ties to the land for both the individual and the group are provided for the following: the !Kung hunters and gatherers of the Kalahari bush of Namibia; the Fulani pastoralists of the savannah and Sahel in West Africa; and the yam cultivators of the forests of Ghana and Nigeria.

These readings are drawn from a typical diversity of African cultures and all tell the story of a human and cultural diversity that matches the environmental diversity. They show both the richness of traditional African cultures and their relevance for today. They clearly show how without an understanding of the African mystical relationship with land non-Africans may continue to misinterpret such traditions as the use of cattle as a bride-price, which to Africans symbolizes the respect and sacrifice that should govern all human relationships, raising the social good above that of the individual.

STUDY FOCUS QUESTIONS

As you complete this week's assignments, consider the following questions.

- How might geographical factors help account for the many contributions that Africa has made to the outside world?
- What are some of the economic adaptations that Africans have made to their various environments?
- Given the indigenous African attitude toward the land, what kinds of conflicts do you see arising from Western intervention, such as the slaughter of game for profit, or the willingness and ability to change whole environments through modern technology?

KEY CONCEPTS AND NAMES

adaptation
Kalahari Desert
Nile River
hunters and gatherers
nomads
pastoralists
rain variability
Rift Valley
vegetation zones
Sahel
Sahara Desert
savannah

QUESTIONS FOR REVIEW

1. Describe some of the factors which determine why certain areas of Africa developed civilizations and others did not.

2. Why are modern Africa's urban populations vulnerable to the impact of environmental stress and in what ways is this stress exhibited?

3. Compare and contrast some of the different ways in which farmers and nomadic pastoralists adapt to the landscapes in which they live.

4. Drought in Africa is not a new phenomenon. Discuss the ways in which rainfall variability affected human society in the past.

5. What different aspects of the environment constrain development in Africa?

ADDITIONAL RECOMMENDED READINGS

Achebe, Chinua. *Things Fall Apart*. New York: Fawcett, 1978.

Buckle, C. *Landforms in Africa*. London: Longman, 1977.

Clark, J. I. (ed.). *An Advanced Geography of Africa*. London: Hulton Educational, 1970.

Deng, Francis Mading. *The Dinka of the Sudan*. New York: Holt, Rinehart and Winston, 1972.

Goldschmidt, W. *Culture and Behavior of the Sebei: A Study in Continuity and Adaptation*. Berkeley: University of California Press, 1976.

Lee, R. B., and I. DeVore (eds.). *Kalahari Hunters-Gatherers: Studies of the !Kung San and Their Neighbors*. Cambridge: Harvard University Press, 1976.

WEEK 4

The Triple Heritage of Lifestyles

OBJECTIVES

After reading this week's assignments and viewing the related program, you should be able to:

- Define and give examples of romantic primitivism and romantic gloriana;
- Identify basic characteristics of Africanity, Islam, and Western Christendom as they exist in Africa;
- Discuss the impact of Islamic and Western customs on the traditional family, identifying the inherent conflicts between African matrilinealism and Western and Islamic patrilinealism;
- Explain the concepts of descent and kinship and the role of ancestors in Africanity and discuss their importance.

STUDY RESOURCES

Check with your instructor for specific assignments.

Television Program
    2. "The Triple Heritage of Lifestyles"
The Africans: A Reader
    Chapter 2, "The Triple Heritage of Lifestyles"
    by Elliott P. Skinner
The Africans: A Triple Heritage by Ali A. Mazrui
    Chapter 4, "The Semitic Impact"
    Chapter 5, "The Western Aftermath"

TELEVISION PROGRAM

This program explores the effects of indigenous, Islamic, and Western cultures on African social organization and lifestyles. These three influences are observed in the lives of cultivators and nomads, and in the roles taken by families and children. Young Africans' influence is seen in the shaping of leisure culture, including sports, the arts, and music. The program also contrasts the historical perspectives of romantic gloriana and romantic primitivism. The former emphasizes periods and places where there have been complex civilizations in Africa. Romantic primitivism, on the other hand, validates simpler, nontechnical traditions.

STUDY FOCUS by Colin M. Turnbull

Throughout this series the central theme that is discussed concerns Africa's triple heritage and how it is evidenced in political, economic, and social life in Africa today. Professor Mazrui, himself a Muslim, is particularly qualified not only to present the history of Islam's introduction and assimilation into Africa, but also to provide an Islamic point of view. But Professor Mazrui simultaneously represents the other legacies as well – through his Kenyan upbringing and his Western education. These legacies can be dissected for the purpose of analysis – as they are throughout the series – but the real story of Africa today, as well as its history, lies in the coexistence of these three traditions and in Africa's search for cultural synthesis.

A second major theme addressed both in this program and throughout the series concerns change: a land that is changing, people who are changing (even genetically through population movement and intermarriage), and cultures that are changing. One key to understanding these changes lies in the ancient, pervasive, and enduring traditional relationship of the peoples of Africa to the land that gives them life. The traditional attachment to family and land not only made the Ashanti what they were, for example, but made it possible for them to resist foreign control and to preserve their identity throughout the creation of the modern state of Ghana.

A third major concept concerns Africans' enormous capacity for adaptation. The coming of two powerful religious forces, Christianity and Islam, initiated radical forms of change; but, as we begin to see here, the triple heritage is not so much one of the domination by one cultural tradition over another as it is one of adaptation and assimilation.

The different cultures shown in this program also cause us to consider the diversity that is and has been Africa and to consider the similarities and contrasts between different African societies of the past and the present.

Professor Skinner's chapter in the text compares and contrasts the basic characteristics and impact of the three religious legacies that have influenced contemporary Africa – Africanity, Islam, and Western Christendom. It also explores the link between the natural and supernatural, one of the more basic characteristics of Africanity, and discusses such significant rites of passage as childbirth, puberty, marriage, and death.

Among the rites of puberty, the chapter discusses circumcision and clitoridectomy, terms that may be unfamiliar. Professor Skinner finds that circumcision of men and clitoridectomy of women are traceable as far back into African history as the Pharaonic period of ancient Egypt. Both are rites performed at puberty, and are part of the initiation rites by which a boy or girl becomes a man or woman. Circumcision is the excision of the foreskin of the male penis, and clitoridectomy is the excision of the clitoris in the female. The exact nature of the latter operation varies from society to society. In a few populations, just the tip of the clitoris is excised; sometimes the whole clitoris is removed; and sometimes infibulation is practiced – in which the edges of the vulva are fastened together leaving only one orifice at the bottom for the exit of urine. In thinking about these practices, it is important to recognize that circumcision is entirely the province of males – not even the initiate's mother has any part in it. And likewise, clitoridectomy is entirely the domain of women – the operation is performed by women upon girls to make them into women, and in traditional societies is accompanied by a period of seclusion and instruction.

In the Africans' view, circumcision and clitoridectomy are counterparts. A myth of the Dogon of Mali explains the practices by saying that when God made human beings He didn't complete the job; He made men with some female characteristics and women with some male characteristics. When human beings make themselves, however, they turn a child into an adult by removing the part that belongs to the other sex. As among Jewish people, there are some African societies that practice male circumcision but no female excision; however, none have clitoridectomy and not circumcision. To Professor Skinner, this suggests that circumcision is the older practice and that clitoridectomy arose among women as an assertion of female equality.

Primary source readings accompanying the chapter are excerpted from: Jomo Kenyatta, *Facing Mount Kenya*; H. A. R. Gibb (trans.), *Ibn*

Battuta: Travels in Asia and Africa 1325-1354; and Erasto Muga, *African Response to Western Christian Religion*.

STUDY FOCUS QUESTIONS

As you complete this week's assignments, consider the following questions.

- In what different ways have Islam and Christianity sought to impress their ideals on indigenous Africa, and with what results?
- How far is the triple heritage a fusion into one single heritage rather than a coexistence of three separate heritages?
- How could the traditional attachment to family and land strengthen the Africans against foreign domination?

KEY CONCEPTS AND NAMES

birth rituals
circumcision
clitoridectomy
divine kingship
imam
jihad
mahdi
polygyny
purdah
Sharia

QUESTIONS FOR REVIEW

1. Describe those factors which make for the enduring nature of ancestral veneration despite Islamization, Christianization, and modernization in African societies.

2. How can one explain the transformation of African independent churches from institutions formed in reaction to the chauvinism of Western Christendom to recognized churches in contemporary Africa?

3. If *jihad* provided the rationale for Islamic expansionism at an earlier point, then in what ways does the growth of modern Islamic cults in Nigeria and Libya appear as a similar or dissimilar process?

4. What traditional or Islamic reinforcements are there for Western notions of "democracy" or "justice" in contemporary African societies?

5. How is the provision of modern education for African women likely to affect their attitudes toward their traditional roles, as well as their roles in Islamic culture?

ADDITIONAL RECOMMENDED READINGS

Gibb, H. A. R. (trans.). *Ibn Battuta: Travels in Asia and Africa 1325-1354*. Fairfield, N.J.: Augustus M. Kelley Publishers, 1929.

Gugler, J., and W. G. Flanagan. *Urbanization and Social Change in West Africa*. Cambridge: Cambridge University Press, 1978.

Hodgkin, Thomas. *Nigerian Perspectives*. London: Oxford University Press, 1975.

Jahn, Janheinz. *Through African Doors*. New York: Grove Press, Inc., 1962.

Kenyatta, Jomo. *Facing Mount Kenya: The Tribal Life of the Gikuyu*. New York: Random House, 1962.

Lipsky, G. A. *Ethiopia: Its People, Its Society, Its Culture*. New Haven: Yale University Press, 1962.

Muga, Erasto. *African Response to Western Christian Religion*. Kampala: The East African Literature Bureau, 1975.

WEEK 5

New Gods

OBJECTIVES

After reading this week's assignments and viewing the related television program, you should be able to:

- Identify the time and method by which Islam and Christianity came to Africa;
- Discuss the impact that traditional African religions have had on Christianity and Islam;
- Discuss the impact that Islam and Christianity have had on traditional African religions, citing several examples of the fusion of the different religions.

STUDY RESOURCES

Check with your instructor for specific assignments.

Television Program
    3. "New Gods"
The Africans: A Reader
    Chapter 3, "New Gods"
    by Lamin Sanneh
The Africans: A Triple Heritage by Ali A. Mazrui
    Chapter 7, "Africa at Prayer"

TELEVISION PROGRAM

This program examines the factors that influence religion in Africa, paying particular attention to the relationship between man and God and to how traditional African religions, Islam, and Christianity coexist and influence each other. It also explores ways in which Christianity and Islam are becoming Africanized, and examines their impact on African languages, laws, and learning.

STUDY FOCUS by Colin M. Turnbull

In the early weeks of the series we have seen something of the all-pervasive attachment of Africans to the land and the family. While neither the worship of nature nor the worship of family even begins to describe the depth and complexity of any one traditional African religion, the two concepts point to central values that are incorporated in all African religions. Another term, *animism*, points to a third critical element. Animism is frequently misinterpreted as meaning that traditional Africans invest objects, animals, or plants with supernatural powers or see them as the abode of spirits. Actually animism refers to belief in a vital force that permeates and animates all things. It is a force that can work on its own or can be manipulated by humans for good or for ill. This spiritual force is as central in African religious thought as the concept of God is in other religious systems. This aspect of their beliefs is directly related to the fact that in Africa religion is seen as a force to be reckoned with every day, in all activities, however mundane.

This week's program shows how the history of Islam and Christianity in Africa is much more complex than merely the history of two missionary endeavors. It is largely a history of traders, travelers, and explorers from two different faiths coming into contact with a third culture that was equally religious but which had a totally different focus. The indigenous focus was on the present rather than the past or future and concerned itself more with relationships among humans than with relationships between humans and God.

Nevertheless, Christianity and Islam have become widely dispersed throughout Africa. Factors that contributed to that spread include trade; war; and, especially in the case of Islam, intermarriage. Although colonialism brought Islam into alliance with indigenous Africa, making it appear more successful than Christianity, in fact, neither new religion was more successful. Each was being adapted, absorbed, and assimilated by a powerful indigenous African tradition. Both foreign religious movements, however, opened doors that gave Africa access to an outside world of which it was destined to become a vital part.

Much of what came into Africa through those open doors was disastrous from many perspectives. But Islam did bring with it a powerful educational system, establishing schools and universities wherever it spread; and it also brought the *Sharia* (Islamic law). Both institutions helped to provide a common meeting ground in periods when political horizons were rapidly expanding. And Islam also opened new avenues for economic as well as cultural exchange.

Similarly, Christianity opened up new horizons and, albeit unintentionally, provided Africans with access to a powerful weapon that was to support their eventual struggle for independence. Much of the revolutionary doctrine that was preached by the independence movements either had its origins in Christian philosophy or found justification there. The sectarian process of fission within the Christian church itself seemed to provide a ready model for the growing number of separatist African Christian movements, many of which became prominent in the fight for independence. Thanks to its Africanization, Christianity has taken on a new importance in Africa, alive with the sounds of African music, with the movement of African dance, and with the vivid imagery and symbolism of the African aesthetic. Islam, too, has become more flexible in the sub-Saharan environment – less doctrinaire and more alive with what Muslims consider the forbidden imagery – imagery that is found at the heart of African religious life.

In his chapter in the text, Professor Sanneh identifies and describes indigenous African religions and analyzes their impact on Islam and Christianity. He also discusses the impact of Islam and Christianity on traditional religions and explains why and how these religions were adopted in Africa, stressing Africa's role in their assimilation.

The primary source readings are a prayer from John S. Mbiti's *The Prayers of African Religion,* and two selections from Edward Evans Evans-Pritchard's *Nuer Religion,* one on the concept of God, the other on sacrifice.

STUDY FOCUS QUESTIONS

As you complete this week's assignments, consider the following questions.

- In what ways has Islam been successful in Africa, and in what ways has it failed to achieve its goals?

- What are the relationships between Christianity and the African religious and political independence movements?
- What are the fundamental differences between indigenous African religion and Islam and Christianity? What are some areas of agreement?

KEY CONCEPTS AND NAMES

hajj
independency
intermarriage
missions
organized religious societies
Sufism
Sunni Islamic Orthodoxy
syncretism
ulama
vernacular translation

QUESTIONS FOR REVIEW

1. Africa now has a plurality of religious paradigms existing sometimes in parallel but at other times in tension with local values and traditions. Discuss the ways in which, in your view, these paradigms promote or challenge earlier conceptions and practice.

2. Christianity was "translated" into African terms long before the era of formal vernacular translation. Yet the strong Western cultural supports of the religion made it relatively resistant to local assimilation. Assess this dual aspect of the religion, showing which is stronger.

3. Christian Africa has the paradox of mission allying itself with colonialism and, on the other hand, stimulating cultural and political nationalism by its vernacular research and translation. Could it be said that in the long run mission and colonialism were destined to diverge in their effects?

4. Possessing the Arabic revelation of the Koran which may not, in canonical rules, be translated, Islam represents an anti-indigenous force. Yet historically it has been adapted into a variety of contexts in Africa and elsewhere. Evaluate this double legacy of the religion.

5. Muslims in Africa may be divided into militants and accommodationists, although in fact accommodation may be said to be more widespread and of deeper significance than militancy. Assess this characterization of the religion, saying which you would stress more.

6. How significant do you think are the indigenous concepts of God and the practice and understanding of sacrifice in Africa? Do you think Christianity or Islam is better placed to assimilate and reinforce such materials?

ADDITIONAL RECOMMENDED READINGS

Evans-Pritchard, E. E. *Nuer Religion*. New York: Oxford at the Clarendon Press, 1940.

Evans-Pritchard, E. E. *Witchcraft, Oracles and Magic Among the Azande*. New York: Oxford at the Clarendon Press, 1937.

Gibb, H. A. R. (trans.). *Ibn Battuta: Travels in Asia and Africa 1325-1354*. Boston: Routledge and Kegan Paul, Ltd., 1929.

Griaule, Marcel. *Conversations with Ogotemmêli: An Introduction to Dogon Religious Ideas*. New York: Oxford University Press, 1965.

Lienhardt, Godfrey. *Divinity and Experience: The Religion of the Dinka*. New York: Oxford at the Clarendon Press, 1961.

Mbiti, John S. *The Prayers of African Religion*. Maryknoll, N.Y.: Orbis Books, 1976.

Muga, Erasto. *African Response to Western Christian Religion*. Kampala: East African Literature Bureau, 1975.

WEEK 6

Exploitation

OBJECTIVES

After reading this week's assignments and viewing the related television program, you should be able to:

- Discuss the impact that Shaka and Usuman dan Fodio had on sub-Saharan Africa;
- Discuss the role of Africans in the slave trade;
- Identify the participants in, purpose of, and outcome of the Berlin Conference of 1884-85;
- Compare and contrast Africa's relationship with the outside world before and after colonization;
- Identify forms of technological and resource exploitation.

STUDY RESOURCES

Check with your instructor for specific assignments.

Television Program
    4. "Exploitation"
The Africans: A Reader
    Chapter 4, "Exploitation"
    by Robert I. Rotberg
The Africans: A Triple Heritage by Ali A. Mazrui
    Chapter 8, "In Search of Development"

TELEVISION PROGRAM

This program examines the exploitation of Africa's human and natural resources and looks at the result of this exploitation before, during, and after the colonial period. Its central proposition is that Africa has contributed more to Western industrialization than the West has contributed to African development. The program also examines Africa's own traditions of slavery and contrasts them with Arabic and Western forms of slavery.

Whatever benefits the new religions brought, any claims either had to moral superiority were rudely shattered by the harsh realities of slavery and colonialism. The often ruthless and barbaric exploitation of Africans by foreign powers from Arabia and Europe is examined here, including the part that Africans themselves played in it. Before, during, and after colonialism, slavery took on different forms. Indigenous African forms of temporary bondage and serfdom were used to deal with lawbreakers while still allowing them a productive life. Another kind of slavery was practiced in Arabia; and the program compares this with the infinitely more cruel and inhumane slavery practiced in the Americas.

Slavery, however, was not the only form of exploitation. From earliest recorded history, the outside world was fascinated by and anxious to have access to Africa's natural resources. There were some strange exchanges, such as salt for gold, and pieces of paper for ivory. Initially, however, these exchanges satisfied the needs and desires of all parties, and there was a perceived parity in them. During the pre-colonial era, foreign traders, particularly the Europeans, were largely confined to the coastal region; but the age of exploration changed all that. There was, in fact, no real isolation of the vast interior of the continent. The Sahara was crossed by well traveled trade routes, and there was movement back and forth from the center of the continent to each coast, keeping the interior as much in a state of change as the coasts. The changes were not only economic but also religious and, increasingly, political. With the expansion of trade routes, formerly egalitarian, segmentary societies grew into centralized and highly stratified kingdoms. Some of these became increasingly autocratic as the foreign traders began introducing guns, which gave the new rulers access to individual power that they had never had before.

At the same time the outside world was also changing, for the same age of exploration had opened up the New World, with all its potential and all its needs. New tastes were being developed in Europe as new goods were brought home by explorers and long distance traders. Professor Rotberg suggests in his chapter that one of the arch-villains of exploitation was the taste for sugar. As demand for this and other exotic commodities grew, there was a corresponding demand for labor to provide them. Africa proved to be a ready source of such labor in the form of slaves. One of this week's readings is an eye-witness account of some of the horrors involved in the transportation of slaves. Both Muslims and Christians joined in the appalling traffic in humanity. Some Africans, too, joined the slavers – at first in self-preservation, but later for their own profit.

Not only the people were exploited, so was the land. As recognition of the enormous economic resources of the continent spread, what became known as "The Scramble for Africa" began, in which a number of the most prominent nations of Europe appropriated vast areas of Africa, drawing boundaries for their own political and economic convenience without regard for the rights of the people who lived there. These boundaries, most of which ignored ancient and well-accepted divisions, often lumped together under a single colonial government people who did not speak the same language or share the same lifestyle. This planted the seeds for some of the most virulent sources of instability in the post-colonial period.

The Europeans seriously underestimated the power of the African tradition, with its focus on family and land as two of the most sacred parts of the indigenous heritage. This proved to be a major factor in the undoing of foreign domination. When in the course of their exploitation the colonial powers assaulted traditional family systems, if only by supporting the missionaries and legislating against indigenous practices, they were in fact weakening their own position. And when they appropriated land for their own exclusive usage and exploitation, often desecrating sacred areas in the name of progress by building on them or converting them to more profitable usage, they eventually pushed the Africans to a point beyond which adaptation and assimilation were no longer practicable. In Kenya, both family and land issues were among the major causes of the Mau Mau Revolution. The chapter readings offer other examples of insensitive and ill-conceived colonial policies.

Professor Rotberg's chapter discusses the development of the slave trade and the exploitative treatment of slaves. It identifies African states that flourished demographically and economically as a result of the slave trade and examines the role of African merchants in opposing the end of the slave trade in the late eighteenth century. The chapter proceeds with a discussion of European political rivalries that led to the partitioning of Africa at the Berlin Conference of 1884-85 and to the new forms of exploitation that developed as the European presence on the continent increased. The chapter also examines the African generation that grew up during the first half of the twentieth century experiencing only white rule.

Primary source readings for this chapter are excerpted from: Alexander I. Falconbridge, *Account of the Slave Trade on the Coast of Africa*; Heinrich Barth, *Travels and Discoveries in North and Central Africa . . . 1849-1855*; George S. Mwase, *Strike a Blow and Die: A Narrative of Race Relations in Colonial Africa* (Robert I. Rotberg, ed.); André Gide, *Travels in the Congo*; and Jomo Kenyatta, *Facing Mount Kenya*.

STUDY FOCUS QUESTIONS

As you complete this week's assignments, consider the following questions.

- What is the significance of the statement that a whole generation of Africans grew up "that had never known any life other than that ultimately directed by whites"?
- In what ways can it be said that Africa has contributed more to Western industrialization than it has received?
- What are the major features of the triple heritage of slavery?
- What aspects of the indigenous heritage helped protect Africans against slavery and other forms of exploitation?
- What were some of the major policies of colonial powers that have affected present relations between those powers and their former territories?

KEY CONCEPTS AND NAMES

al-hajj Umar
autocratic rule
Cecil Rhodes
centralized kingdoms
charismatic leadership
competitive exploitation
religious purification
Shaka
theocracy
Zulu

QUESTIONS FOR REVIEW

1. Why did whites enslave Africans?
2. What impact did the slave trade have on the peoples of inner Africa?
3. What were the consequences of the African revolutions of the nineteenth century?
4. What role did the European explorers of Africa play in the partition of Africa?
5. Why and how did Europe succeed in carving up black Africa at the end of the nineteenth century?
6. Why were Africans unable to prevent the imposition of imperial rule?

ADDITIONAL RECOMMENDED READINGS

Barth, Heinrich. *Travels and Discoveries in North and Central Africa . . . 1849-1855.* London: F. Cass and Co., Ltd., 1965.

Falconbridge, Alexander I. *Account of the Slave Trade on the Coast of Africa* (c. 1788). New York: AMS Press, Inc., 1973.

Gide, André. *Travels in the Congo.* New York: Alfred A. Knopf, 1929.

Kenyatta, Jomo. *Facing Mount Kenya: The Tribal Life of the Gikuyu.* New York: Random House, 1962.

Mwase, George S. *Strike a Blow and Die: A Narrative of Race Relations in Colonial Africa.* Edited by Robert I. Rotberg. Cambridge: Harvard University Press, 1967.

Palmer, R. *Land and Racial Domination in Rhodesia.* London: Heinemann Educational Books, Ltd., 1977.

Penrose, E. F. (ed.). *European Imperialism and the Partition of Africa.* London: Frank Cass and Co., Ltd., 1975.

WEEK 7

New Conflicts

OBJECTIVES

After reading this week's assignments and viewing the related television program, you should be able to:

- Discuss the effects of the triple heritage on the nationalist movement, the warrior tradition of indigenous Africa, the *jihad* tradition of Islam, and modern guerilla warfare;
- Describe methods used to establish political boundaries in Africa and discuss the conflicts engendered by the implementation of these methods;
- Discuss lineage as an essential element of social organization in Africa;
- Explain how age-grades serve as a means of social solidarity distinct from the extended family;
- Discuss the authority of women under dual-sex systems.

STUDY RESOURCES

Check with your instructor for specific assignments.

Television Program
    5. "New Conflicts"
The Africans: A Reader
    Chapter 5, "New Conflicts"
    by Pearl T. Robinson
The Africans: A Triple Heritage by Ali A. Mazrui
    Chapter 9, "In Search of Stability"

TELEVISION PROGRAM

This program looks at the tensions inherent in the juxtaposition of three heritages, exploring ways in which these conflicts have contributed to the setting of boundaries, urbanization, the warrior tradition of indigenous Africa, the jihad tradition of Islam, modern guerilla warfare, and the nationalist movement. It examines the methods by which outsiders established the boundaries of African colonies without regard to local population patterns, or, in some cases, even geography, and it identifies some of the effects of these boundary decisions.

STUDY FOCUS by Colin M. Turnbull

This week's materials continue the investigation of post-colonial Africa and the problems that arose in response to the triple heritage. The focus this week is on conflicts that arose from the incorporation of an ancient culture with a vast range of highly effective traditional political systems into a totally alien political context. The boundaries drawn by colonial powers often threw together different cultural and linguistic groups that had little in common but their Africanity, and who in the pre-colonial era were relatively independent both politically and economically. Even worse, the colonial powers created political units that were destined to become nations out of an almost impossible diversity of formerly independent systems. The indigenous systems included everything from stateless societies without chiefs or headmen to relatively recent states, kingdoms, and empires for which fixed boundaries were unimportant or even dysfunctional. At all levels, flexibility and adaptability were crucial to success; but the systems the colonial powers introduced, like their boundaries, were anything but flexible.

The materials this week show something of the pre-colonial systems, and how their political structures were based on such diverse principles as lineage, age cohorts, and kingship. These systems were not necessarily mutually exclusive, and indeed frequently overlapped. Kinship was an important principle throughout, even at the state level, providing at least a mythical, idealized model of the state as one family descended from a single ancestor. Where there were no kings or chiefs, lineage often provided a hierarchical system that defined the various necessary areas of authority. Where such specialization was not necessary for political purposes, the concept of family was still used to give political reality to corporate economic groups. In all these systems the focus was on corporate social responsibility rather than on individual authority. The structures were essentially cooperative rather than competitive, but lent themselves to competition and aggression when these elements were introduced. Another vital traditional polity was that based on age. Many populations were divided into age-grades, or levels, with each grade being assigned very specific economic and political responsibilities. As with lineage, age served as an ordered way of dividing essential labor for the good of society as a whole. The initiation rituals that took place throughout the continent attested to the widespread importance of this structure, making the transfer of power predictable, orderly, and public. Political authority was by no means always vested entirely in one age-grade, but was divided so that elders held responsibility over some political issues, while adults or youths had authority in other matters. Such division, as with lineal divisions, provided a major check against the abuse of power.

The traditional chieftaincies and kingships equally were marked by numerous political checks and balances. Even where there were "divine kingships" this by no means meant that the king, being a god, had absolute power and authority. On the contrary, it often placed him under an even heavier burden to prove his worth *as representative* of divine (ancestral) authority, by being as perfect as possible. Further, there were mechanisms for removing rulers when they proved less than perfect.

Sometimes the highly centralized colonial powers tried to make use of traditional chiefs and kings. But where a colonial territory consisted of a wide variety of traditional political structures, the colonials often chose to rule through the one that had the most centralized system, creating tribal jealousies and imbalances that would plague the new nations long after independence. Where no centralized system existed, colonial governments sometimes created them, suddenly inventing and appointing chiefs. This, too, led to innumerable problems when the colonial powers withdrew, leaving behind a conflict-ridden political scene. In her chapter, Professor Robinson discusses the notion of "conflict structures," providing a theoretical basis for analyzing political conflict and showing how conflict is by no means always dysfunctional; it can, indeed, be highly constructive, and not infrequently is a powerful unifying force.

In this chapter, Professor Robinson also examines the foundations of indigenous political systems in Africa in an attempt to analyze structures of later political conflict. Societies based on lineage, age groups, dual-sex authority systems, and kingship are discussed. The chapter explores reasons for the diminished status of women in Africa today and identifies concepts of communalism, patron-client relations, and class affiliations that affect Africa's search for stability.

Primary source readings for this chapter are excerpted from: Pearl T. Robinson, "Traditional Clientage and Political Change in a Hausa Community," from *Transformation and Resiliency in Africa*; Dunston M. Wai, *The African-Arab Conflict in the Sudan*; Ngugi wa Thiong'o, *Petals of Blood*; Ryszard Kapuscinski, *The Emperor: Downfall of an Autocrat*; and Carol Hermer, *The Diary of Maria Tholo*.

STUDY FOCUS QUESTIONS

As you complete this week's assignments, consider the following questions.

- In pre-colonial Africa, how might a society that had no formal state structure be governed?
- Can it be said that the status of African women has invariably improved as a result of Western influences?
- How were African monarchies governed?
- What is a political conflict structure? Which types of structural arrangements are often associated with political conflict in Africa?
- What is meant by the term "class formation"?

KEY CONCEPTS AND NAMES

age cohorts
class formation
clientelism
communalism
dual-sex political systems
fixed territorial borders
Haile Selassie
lineage
stateless societies
stratification

QUESTIONS FOR REVIEW

1. Why is the situation in Chad frequently cited as a classic example of communal conflict?

2. How has the form of indigenous social clientage that exists among the Hausa of Nigeria and Niger been incorporated into politics and the affairs of government in these two states?

3. How has the process of class formation evolved in Kenya?

4. What kinds of structural arrangements did politicians in Tibiri, Niger, rely on to mobilize supporters as they engaged in competitive party politics?

5. What developments led to the buildup of communal conflict in the Sudan?

6. Why was Munira, the protagonist in Ngugi wa Thiong'o's novel *Petals of Blood*, so offended by the events that occurred when he went to the tea hosted by the Kamwene Cultural Organization?

7. Why was it considered dangerous for university students to think about what was going on in imperial Ethiopia?

8. What event provoked the violence that resulted in the death of so many black South African students in 1976? Why did the old man at the funeral insist on paying homage to the children of Gutulu?

ADDITIONAL RECOMMENDED READINGS

Adam, H. *Modernizing Racial Domination: South Africa's Political Dynamics*. Berkeley: University of California Press, 1971.

Carter, G. M., and P. O'Meara (eds.). *Southern Africa in Crisis*. Bloomington: Indiana University Press, 1977.

Dunn, J. (ed.). *African States: Failure and Promise*. Cambridge: Cambridge University Press, 1978.

Hermer, Carol. *The Diary of Maria Tholo*. Johannesburg: Ravan Press, 1980.

Kapuscinski, Ryszard. *The Emperor: Downfall of an Autocrat*. New York: Harcourt Brace Jovanovich, Inc., 1984.

Robinson, Pearl T., and Elliott P. Skinner (eds.). *Transformation and Resiliency in Africa*. Washington, D.C.: Howard University Press, 1983.

Wai, Dunston M. *The African-Arab Conflict in the Sudan*. New York: Africana Publishing Co., 1981.

wa Thiong'o, Ngugi. *Petals of Blood*. New York: E. P. Dutton, 1977.

WEEK 8

In Search of Stability

OBJECTIVES

After reading this week's assignments and viewing the related television program, you should be able to:

- Define and give examples of African one-party states, multi-party states, and socialist states;
- Identify at least three goals of African leaders in the post-independence period;
- Compare and contrast historical and contemporary examples of Africa's search for stability, citing reasons for success or failure;
- Discuss the statement: "Africa is lurching between tyranny and anarchy."

STUDY RESOURCES

Check with your instructor for specific assignments.

Television Program
    6. "In Search of Stability"
The Africans: A Reader
    Chapter 6, "In Search of Stability"
    by Fred M. Hayward
The Africans: A Triple Heritage by Ali A. Mazrui
    Chapter 10, "Is Modernization Reversible?"

TELEVISION PROGRAM

This program depicts and discusses several means of governing, asking which efforts have succeeded, which have failed, and why. Current unrest and new social orders are examined to illustrate an Africa in search of a viable form of government. Examples include Ghana,

Nigeria, and the Sudan. The program explores the differences between Islamic and Westernized military regimes and examines several long-lasting examples of the one-party state.

STUDY FOCUS by Colin M. Turnbull

One of the most fundamental questions raised this week concerns the apparent irony between the greatness and stability traditional Africa has achieved in the past and the fact that to some it appears incapable of similar achievements today. The question does not focus attention only on demographic or technological issues, as important as these are; it also compels Westerners to question their own concepts of success and failure, and even the very concept of progress by which contemporary Africa is so frequently judged.

Westerners tend to see both time and space as linear, whereas in most African traditions time is viewed as cyclical. Looked at cyclically, the very notion of African progress over a specific period of time becomes difficult to judge. And so when this unit compares the initial economic and political successes of some of the first African nations to win independence with their subsequent decline into seeming anarchy, when it examines how in recent times tyrants have sometimes supplanted good, democratic leaders, there is a need to be wary of seeing this as necessarily being a *decline*. For one thing, violence and bloodshed are often overemphasized at the expense of the less spectacular success stories. But in any case, the decay of social institutions, like the decay of physical objects, should be assessed in terms of their utility in specific contexts.

African traditional cultures are essentially pragmatic. It is part of their adaptive genius that a ruler's worth is measured strictly by the success with which he rules. In many traditional kingdoms the kings were granted seemingly absolute power, but were regarded not so much as divine in themselves as receptacles for ancestral authority and power. When their rule failed to fulfill the will of the people, there were mechanisms for their removal and replacement by someone more fit. Thus, it is not the theory of democracy that is important in choosing one form of government over another. Nor is it important whether the leader does or does not wear a uniform. The prime consideration is whether or not the system will work as the people want it to work.

Other social institutions are similarly treated: their value is assessed by how well or badly they work. Polygyny, for instance, might have worked well in the past – and indeed, might still work well in rural areas with a subsistence economy – yet be economically disastrous in an urban context. This would not be viewed as a contradiction within Africa, as each value would be correct in the context in which it was operative.

Caution is also called for in judging individual actions by Western values, for what may appear to be greed and corruption by Western standards may be seen very differently in Africa. In traditional societies a ruler's worth was often symbolized by his wealth, for his wealth was the wealth of the nation. He was also meant to be as all powerful as he was all wealthy. These values have sometimes persisted in systems that are essentially democratic as we understand the term.

Examples of different post-colonial approaches to stability include one-party systems, multi-party systems, and revolutionary systems. Despite this diversity of approaches, certain common and essentially traditional African elements make themselves apparent. For instance, individual freedom does not rank high, dedication to the state is paramount, and the voluntary labor of men and women in the fields may far outrank money in terms of national wealth.

In looking for democracy at work in Africa today, one should not be too easily put off by outward appearances of autocracy, though the very real abuses and tragedies that some of the new African nations have suffered at the hands of the very real tyrants should not be dismissed. But such tyranny did not derive from traditional origins. The whole modern concept of a nation-state in a global arena, with a highly specialized and powerful ruling class, was something totally foreign to traditional Africa. Nobody foresaw just how difficult it would be for Africans to take control of the new political units that the colonial powers had arbitrarily created.

In his chapter, Professor Hayward discusses the immediate post-independence period of experimentation. He examines the efforts of the newly independent African states to create a new order by building on what had been achieved elsewhere, but hoping to avoid some of the pit-falls of other states. Examined here are the excitement of this period, the new nationalism, and the efforts to create, build, and assert the impor-tance and significance of Africa at home and in the world political arenas. The text describes one-party states, African socialism, and military rule, identifying examples of successes and failures. Military intervention, the demise of multi-party competition in many states, the problems of national integration, the widespread loss of civil liberties, and the difficulties of institution-building and development also are discussed.

The primary source readings for this chapter are excerpted from: *The New York Times,* "Gold Coast Seeks Lead in Industry"; Nelson Mandela, "Black Man in a White Court," from *No Easy Walk to Freedom*; Julius K. Nyerere, "The Policy of Self-Reliance," from *Freedom and Socialism: A Selection from Writings and Speeches, 1965-1967*; and Kwame Nkrumah, *Revolutionary Path.*

STUDY FOCUS QUESTIONS

As you complete this week's assignments, consider the following questions.

- What is the role of "family" in determining wealth?
- How are sharing and cooperation, and competition and hoarding, valued by each segment of the triple heritage?
- How is freedom defined in the modern nations?
- What has been the influence of money and a cash economy on indigenous African values?

KEY CONCEPTS AND NAMES

cultural relativism
Houphouet-Boigny
Jomo Kenyatta
Kuba
Nelson Mandela
Kwame Nkrumah
Julius Nyerere
Jerry Rawlings
ujamaa village

QUESTIONS FOR REVIEW

1. Discuss self-reliance as spelled out in the Arusha Declaration. What were its goals, requirements, and meaning?
2. Both Ghana and Tanzania talked about establishing African socialism. How do their programs differ, especially as spelled out in the

readings by Nkrumah and Nyerere? Which do you find to be the most likely to succeed?

3. What are the differences between the systems of government in independent Ethiopia and Sierra Leone? Which do you think was the most successful? Why?

4. What were the causes of the breakdown of law and order in the Congo? What might have been done to prevent it?

5. What explains the growing incidence of military rule in Africa? How is it justified? What changes result from it? How do you evaluate the results?

6. What problems do Algeria, Guinea-Bissau, and South Africa have in common?

7. Assess the period of political experimentation, noting its successes and failures. Which experiments do you find to be the most promising? Why?

ADDITIONAL RECOMMENDED READINGS

Afrifa, A. A. *The Ghana Coup: 24th February 1966.* London: Frank Cass and Company, 1966.

Apter, David. *Ghana in Transition.* New York: Atheneum Press, 1983.

Armah, Ayi Kwei. *The Beautyful Ones Are Not Yet Born.* Boston: Houghton Mifflin, 1968.

Bay, Edna (ed.). *Women and Work in Africa.* Boulder: Westview Press, 1982.

Brain, James. "Less Than Second Class Citizens: Women in Ujamaa Villages in Tanzania," in N. Hafkin and E. Bay (eds.), *Women in Africa: Studies in Social and Economic Change.* Stanford: Stanford University Press, 1976.

Cabral, Amilcar. *Revolution in Guinea.* New York: Monthly Review Press, 1969.

Finer, S. E. *The Man on Horseback: The Role of the Military in Politics.* Middlesex: Penguin Books, 1962.

Foster, Philip, and Aristide R. Zolberg. *Ghana and the Ivory Coast: Perspectives on Modernization.* Chicago: University of Chicago Press, 1971.

"Gold Coast Seeks Lead in Industry," *The New York Times,* May 15, 1955.

Greenfield, Richard. *Ethiopia: A New Political History*. London: Pall Mall Press, 1965.

Halpern, Manfred. *The Politics of Social Change in the Middle East and North Africa*. Princeton: Princeton University Press, 1963.

Humbaraci, Arslan. *Algeria: A Revolution that Failed: A Political History Since 1954*. New York: Praeger, 1966.

Mandela, Nelson. *No Easy Walk to Freedom*. London: Heinemann Educational Books, 1965.

Nkrumah, Kwame. *Revolutionary Path*. New York: International Publishers, 1973.

Nyerere, Julius K. *Freedom and Socialism: A Selection from Writings and Speeches 1965-1967*. Oxford: Oxford University Press, 1968.

Urdang, Stephanie. "Women in Contemporary National Liberation Movements," in M. Hay (ed.), *African Women: South of the Sahara*. London and New York: Longman, 1984.

Young, M. Crawford, *Politics in the Congo*. Princeton: Princeton University Press, 1965.

Zolberg, Aristide. *One Party Government in the Ivory Coast*. Princeton: Princeton University Press, 1964.

WEEK 9

A Garden of Eden in Decay?

OBJECTIVES

After reading this week's assignments and viewing the related television program, you should be able to:

- Identify both internal and external decay-producing forces affecting modern Africa;
- Compare and contrast the impact of these decay-producing forces on individuals and societies, and identify attempts to reverse the decay;
- Discuss the notion of appropriate and inappropriate technology in relation to the development of independent African nations;
- Discuss the statement: "Africa produces what it does not consume and consumes what it does not produce";
- Explain why Africa is pulled between dependency and decay.

STUDY RESOURCES

Check with your instructor for specific assignments.

Television Program
　　7. "A Garden of Eden in Decay?"
The Africans: A Reader
　　Chapter 7, "A Garden of Eden in Decay?"
　　by Victor A. Olorunsola
The Africans: A Triple Heritage by Ali A. Mazrui
　　Chapter 11, "In Search of Independence"

TELEVISION PROGRAM

This program shows a continent that is rich in minerals, but one in which famine, deforestation, unharnessed and ill-used water supplies, and an advancing desert are prominent. The theme of the program is that the continent produces what it does not consume and consumes what it does not produce. The program also explores how Africa spends its money, the problems of inappropriate technology donated by outsiders, the inadequacies of the communications systems, and the apparent widespread corruption in business and government.

STUDY FOCUS by Colin M. Turnbull

To non-Africans it often seems that Africa today is in a process of decay. The political systems introduced by colonial powers are crumbling, as are many of the monumental buildings constructed to house colonial and post-independence governments. Many highly sophisticated technological systems are sitting idle, similarly decaying. But, as the program shows, that technology was often inappropriate, as were some of the political structures that were designed more to maintain control than to achieve growth and development. In light of this, what may seem like decay may not be decay at all. It may just be the face of change as African nations attempt to adapt to a world that has changed all around them.

Among the concerns of this program is the continuing economic exploitation of African countries following their independence, a situation that drove some African governments to the conclusion that it was better to be poor as a result of their own mistakes than because of exploitation by others. While the program raises doubts as to whether there ever truly was a state of Eden in Africa, it makes clear that the indigenous traditions were highly effective *in their specific contexts*, at least, and had a resilience and adaptivity that enabled them to persist through time. For example, the use of traditional technologies has persisted, but precolonial subsistence economies used technology to achieve adequacy, treating both surplus and deficit as equal evils. The transition to the use of more modern technology and to different economic goals may have been just too great, and the time too short, for the sure, steady, and slow process of adaptation to make success possible.

Pre-colonial Africa may not have been a Garden of Eden, but the traditional economic systems encouraged each person to produce what he or she needed for consumption. Today, notes Mazrui, "Africa produces what it does not consume, and consumes what it does not produce." Further, in the past each political system had recognized, accepted rules of conduct that were supported by an intricate system of religious beliefs and practices rather than by rules of force. Both the political and the economic technologies the new nations inherited from the West have challenged the traditional orders but have not replaced them with mechanisms that work well for Africans.

This program encourages consideration of charges of corruption and nepotism that are frequently leveled against contemporary African governments and individuals. These, too, need to be evaluated against both traditional and colonial history and examined in the context of a traditional morality that demands reciprocity, family support, and the responsiblity of those in power to amass wealth for distribution to the needy in times of crisis. There is now a dramatic conflict between the pull of the old, essentially social, communal, family-oriented heritage, and the much more individual, success-oriented push of the colonial heritage.

While individual governments are devising their own solutions, they are also working with each other. This week's materials discuss such interaction among the new nations of Africa. Such cooperation shows the resilience and power of the indigenous tradition, working harmoniously with the Islamic and Christian elements of the triple heritage. It is essentially African that African nations join together to tackle the problems facing them by calling for ethical codes of conduct, placing a clearly traditional priority on morality over legality.

Professor Olorunsola's chapter considers the economic history of the continent and analyzes causes of the current economic state. The notion of appropriate and inappropriate technology in relation to the development of independent African states is discussed, and criteria for appropriate technology decisions are suggested. The author identifies such decay-producing forces as inefficiency and mismanagement, corruption, inadequate and inappropriate education, uneven development, and exploitation by multinational corporations and foreign companies. The effect of these problems on individuals is discussed and attempts to reverse the decay are examined, including the establishment of ethical codes of conduct, the Lagos Plan of Action, small scale industrial development, and food policies. Primary source readings for this chapter are excerpted from: United Nations Economic Commission for Africa, "Development and Economic Cooperation: Proposals for Consideration by African Governments," from *Economic Bulletin for Africa*; and Adebayo Adedeji, "Implementation of the Strategies and Plan of Action at the International Global Level," from *After Lagos What?*

STUDY FOCUS QUESTIONS

As you complete this week's assignments, consider the following questions.

- In what ways are the demands being made by some East African governments for rules for ethical conduct reflected in the Lagos Plan of Action?
- How can the triple heritage be seen at work in issues such as corruption and nepotism? Consider both the individual elements of the triple heritage and the heritage as a whole.
- List some of the causes of "decay," both external and internal, in the four major areas of social life: domestic, economic, political, and religious.

KEY WORDS AND CONCEPTS

appropriate technology
brain drain
displaced labor
external debt
Lagos Plan of Action
levels of investment
life expectancy at birth
patron-client relationships
per capita food production
price policies
rural-urban drift

QUESTIONS FOR REVIEW

1. Discuss reasons for the present economic conditions in Africa with regard to: food production; external debt; birthrate; and literacy.

2. To what extent have the structures of colonial economies, transformation of African economies, and the competitive international economic system contributed to the economic conditions in Africa today?

3. What factors should be considered in determining whether a type of technology is appropriate or inappropriate for Africa?

4. Discuss the possible impact of Africa's current economic state on groups of individuals, such as parents and the educated elite.

5. Given the dependency of African economies on the international economic order, in your opinion what are the prospects for African economic development in the future?

ADDITIONAL RECOMMENDED READINGS

Adedeji, Adebayo. "Implementation of the Strategies and the Plan of Action at the International Global Level," in *After Lagos What?* Tripoli: The African Centre for Applied Research and Training in Social Development, 1983.

Brett, A. E. *Colonialism and Underdevelopment in East Africa.* New York: Nork Publishers, 1973.

Diwan, K. R., and D. Livingstone. *Alternative Development Strategies and Appropriate Technology.* New York: Pergamon Press, 1979.

Ekpo, U. M. (ed.). *Bureaucratic Corruption in Sub-Saharan Africa.* Washington, D.C.: University Press of America, 1977.

Food and Agriculture Organization. *Famine in Africa.* Rome: FAO, 1982.

Schumacher, E. F. *Small Is Beautiful.* London: Blond and Briggs, 1983.

United Nations. *Appropriate Technology and Research for Industrial Development.* New York: United Nations, 1972.

United Nations Economic Commission for Africa. "Development and Economic Cooperation: Proposals for Consideration by African Governments." *Economic Bulletin for Africa* 11(1977):2.

Watts, M. *Silent Violence: Food, Famine, and Peasantry in Northern Nigeria.* Los Angeles: University of California Press, 1983.

World Bank. *Accelerated Development in Sub-Saharan Africa: An Agenda for Action.* Washington, D.C.: The World Bank, 1984.

—— WEEK 10 ——

A Conflict of Cultures

OBJECTIVES

After reading this week's assignments and viewing the related television program, you should be able to:

- Identify and discuss conflicts that have arisen as a result of the interaction of the three legacies, citing examples that relate to women, the law, education, and urbanization;
- Discuss the changing nature of women's roles and status, citing specific Islamic, non-Islamic, traditional, and nontraditional examples.

STUDY RESOURCES

Check with your instructor for specific assignments.

Television Program
    8. "A Conflict of Cultures"
The Africans: A Reader
    Chapter 8, "A Conflict of Cultures"
    by Elliott P. Skinner
    and Gwendolyn Mikell
The Africans: A Triple Heritage by Ali A. Mazrui
    Chapter 12, "In Search of Synthesis"

TELEVISION PROGRAM

This program is concerned with values and more specifically, a fusion of values. It explores how modern Africans reconcile the often contradictory signals they receive from their triple heritage, and it depicts the coexistence of traditional practices and rituals with modern activities. Professor Mazrui looks at the public tribunals in Ghana and Kenya, and at the ways in which customary law, Western law, and the Sharia are often at odds on such issues as inheritance. In the Sudan, the program follows the debate over Islamic law and its effectiveness in reducing crime.

STUDY FOCUS by Colin M. Turnbull

In some parts of Africa, and at some times, the various elements of the triple heritage have so grown together and assumed such traditional African form as to be indistinguishable from one another. Members of one religious group even join other religious groups in the practice of their rites and celebration of their festivities — a situation which elsewhere, or at other times, could be considered heresy and punished. But in Africa this intermingling, almost amounting to a fusion, is a source of enormous strength. It enables Africa to deal equally, and as equals, with both the Muslim and the Christian worlds.

On occasion, however, there is conflict when the three systems confront each other; and this is particularly true in the area of law. Unlike in the colonial period, when the Western-style court always had the final say, in today's Africa complications abound due to the coexistence of different legal systems. Western law and Islamic law are at odds over such questions as inheritance. And women's rights are proving to be a central issue, though for different reasons than are generally expressed in the Western world. In some African nations faith is being placed exclusively in the Western system, while other governments are insisting on the exclusive acceptance of the Sharia, or are anxious to get rid of all foreign elements. In Tanzania we see how a tribe that long ago adopted Islam is now rejecting both foreign elements of the triple heritage and attempting to revert to an earlier system of matrilineal descent and inheritance. Where instability and conflict have peaked, central governments are no longer able to govern remote regions effectively. In some nations, such as Zaire, Africanity has revived and taken control as much by default as by policy.

While Islam has attempted to enforce its own value system wherever it was prevalent, on the whole it was much more readily assimilated into the traditional religious system than was Western Christendom. Further, because Western Christendom arrived with the military power and exploitative zeal of the European colonials, it forced Islam and indigenous

Africa into alliance. Also a divisive factor was the fact that with colonial power behind it Christianity was able to penetrate every nook and cranny of African societies, incorporating them into the international world.

Western colonial powers, imbued with their own sense of superiority, remained profoundly and often willfully ignorant of the values of the people they ruled. To a lesser extent, the same was true of the Islamic invaders who sought to impose their way by *jihad*, or holy war. Today many Africans still living in rural areas relatively untouched by either Islamization or Westernization remain ignorant about the realities of the wider world of which they are now an essential economic and political part. And even where education has spread under African rule it is often difficult to create a sense of nationhood and to convey a sense of responsibility to a global brotherhood of nations. In that wider perspective, groups that encourage large families, economies geared to adequacy rather than surplus, and political systems that are inward rather than outward looking may create ongoing conflicts in the overall effort to achieve some measure of cultural synthesis. The traditional subtle art of compromise is the characteristically adaptive force that will, if anything can, make a single reality out of the triple heritage and so resolve the conflict of cultures.

In the text chapter, Professors Skinner and Mikell discuss a variety of conflicts and contradictions facing contemporary African states. The chapter begins with a discussion of the inherent conflicts in cultures and some of the ways in which cultures change. Through an examination of time, economics, marriage, and education, the chapter explores attitudes toward polygyny, bride-price, childrearing, Christian versus Muslim education, and art.

The primary source readings accompanying this chapter are excerpted from: Wole Soyinka, *Aké: The Years of Childhood*; J. Sorie Conteh, "Circumcision and Secret Societies," from *West Africa*; Georges Balandier, *Ambiguous Africa: Cultures in Collision*; Judith Miller, "Egypt's Assembly Bars Full Islamic Law," from *The New York Times*; and Freda Wolfson, *Pageant of Ghana*.

STUDY FOCUS QUESTIONS

As you complete this week's assignments, consider the following questions.

- How might indigenous values have a special advantage in a modern context such as urbanization and the creation of slums?
- In what ways have each of the three heritages favored accommodation, acculturation, or synthesis?
- What is the cultural significance of clitoridectomy? How is its significance changing under pressure to modernize?
- What contemporary problems in Africa are fundamentally educational and cultural rather than political or economic?

KEY CONCEPTS AND NAMES

lobolo
matrilineality
Négritude
palaver
patrilineality
Signares
voluntary associations

QUESTIONS FOR REVIEW

1. As modernization continues in Africa, would you expect to see a resolution of cultural conflict in favor of any one of the three cultural traditions? Explain why.

2. Was African independence sufficient to alter the native self-image which was generally a legacy of Western domination? Give reasons for your answer.

3. Can we ascribe the phenomenal rate of urbanization in modern Africa to reasons other than the Islamic-based urban tradition, in combination with the colonially derived emphasis on urban jobs and education? Explain.

4. Will Africanization of Islam help or hinder Africa as its people continue to develop by making use of modern education?

5. Given the experiences Africans have had with alien ideologies, what factors would now persuade them to accept new alien ideologies or convince them of the need to develop novel indigenous ones?

ADDITIONAL RECOMMENDED READINGS

Balandier, Georges. *Ambiguous Africa: Cultures in Collision.* New York: Pantheon Books of Random House, 1966.

Conteh, J. Sorie. "Circumcision and Secret Societies," *West Africa.* August 18, 1980.

Fraser, D., and H. Cole (eds.). *African Art and Leadership.* Madison: University of Wisconsin Press, 1972.

Gugler, J., and W. G. Flanagan. *Urbanization and Social Change in West Africa.* Cambridge: Cambridge University Press, 1978.

Oppong, C. *Marriage Among a Matrilineal Elite, a Family Study of Ghanaian Senior Civil Servants.* Cambridge: Cambridge University Press, 1974.

Soyinka, Wole. *Aké: the Years of Childhood.* New York: Random House, 1983.

Soyinka, Wole. *Myth, Literature, and the African World.* Cambridge: Cambridge University Press, 1976.

Turner, H. W. *History of an African Independent Church* (2 vols.). Oxford: Oxford University Press, 1967.

WEEK 11

Africa in the World

OBJECTIVES

After reading this week's assignments and viewing the related television program, you should be able to:

- Compare and contrast Africa's influence in the world 3,000 years ago and today;
- Describe the contemporary African diaspora, differentiating between the process of assimilation of Africans residing in Western cultures and that of Africans residing in Arab cultures;
- Identify African reactions to such movements as Pan-Africanism and Garveyism;
- Describe superpower rivalry in Africa and identify current roles of former colonial powers. Define alignment and nonalignment as they relate to Africa.

STUDY RESOURCES

Check with your instructor for specific assignments.

Television Program
    9. "Africa in the World"
The Africans: A Reader
    Chapter 9, "Africa in the World"
    by Victor T. Le Vine
The Africans: A Triple Heritage by Ali A. Mazrui
    Chapter 13, "Between Society and State"

TELEVISION PROGRAM

This final program looks at Africa's relations with the rest of the world and at the continuing influence of the superpowers on the affairs of the continent. Among the issues it addresses are: Africa's role at the United Nations; the role of such critical resources as cobalt; the importance of the International Monetary Fund; the role of food aid; tourism; Islamic solutions; Africa and the bomb; and problems in South Africa.

STUDY FOCUS by Colin M. Turnbull

From the first week, this series has shown what a dynamic role Africa plays in the world. The continent never has been isolated from the rest of the world, though the nature of the relationship has sometimes changed dramatically from one era to another. While this program focuses primarily on contemporary global political and economic relationships, it also serves as a reminder that today, as in the past, there is vital interchange in cultural, economic, and religious areas.

The role of Africa in the contemporary international community is still misunderstood. As in earlier times, Africa contributes at least as much to the world as it receives. In order to fully understand the role of Africa today, one needs to view the continent as more than a mere recipient. Numerous examples of two-way exchange can be cited. Africans who have gone out into both the East and West to further their education, intent on bringing back all the advantages of a primarily Western education, have often found an unexpected respect for their own cultures. Instead of holding to their former conviction that Westernization of their countries was the way of the future, these Africans came to a realization that Africanization could be equally viable.

Another side to Africa's relations with the world is seen in the relationship between black Americans and their land of origin. Black Americans not only continue to explore their own multiple heritage but they also take an increasingly prominent interest in both the internal politics of Africa and African relations with the United States. It is often suggested that if this force were mobilized and organized it could become a very potent voice in U.S. politics, comparable in influence to that of American Jews. African governments are by no means unaware of this. Just as African Muslims make the religious pilgrimage to Mecca, so do thousands of black American tourists make pilgrimages to their African homeland.

Black American involvement also increasingly affects international economic relations. The continent is a vital source of crucial raw materials. In spite of the steady flow of Africa's enormous riches out into the industrialized world, however, Africa's economic troubles continue. Economic difficulties can be just as repressive as the former political subordination of colonial days; at times almost seeming to be yet another form of exploitation. The Western credit/interest system, largely responsible for the continuing fiscal dependency of many African nations, can be contrasted with the Islamic concept of interest-free loans on a risk/profit-sharing basis. Given the indigenous tradition of cooperation rather than competition, one can understand the attractiveness of the Islamic ideal. Africa's economic arrangements offer yet another example of the complexity of the triple heritage. All three cultures make their own contributions to the contemporary economic scene – and most effectively so when coercion is minimal. Ultimately it is the voice of Africa that will determine economic as well as political issues; and that voice has already demonstrated that there is not going to be a wholesale adoption of any one foreign system, whether economic, political, or religious.

A comparison of Soviet and American attitudes toward Africa reveals that politics cannot be separated from economics any more than it can be separated from religious or social considerations. The Soviets may have been disturbed to find the revolutionary zeal they admired and supported in Africa often resulted in what they might consider the establishment of a bourgeoisie. Western democracies, however, have also been discomfited by the emergence of so many one-party systems and apparent autocracies in Africa. Superpower involvement in Africa is portrayed as being as strong as ever, but this week's program also points out that the new African nations are working out their own individual destinies in their own essentially African manner.

While contemplation of the continent's political future raises many questions, the biggest question of all remains the continued presence of white-ruled South Africa, and of its racially dominated policies that could, if not drastically changed, alter the entire political scene almost overnight. This week's program and chapter examine the ongoing battle against the racial policies of South Africa. For instance, a worldwide protest movement has influenced U.S. policy and brought about some divestiture of U.S. investments in South Africa, which, however controversial economically, makes a powerful political and moral statement. The condemnation of South Africa at the United Nations by the newly independent African nations, and other international political anti-apartheid actions that have led to the virtual exclusion of South Africa from international sports, are also shown to be significant.

In his chapter, Professor Le Vine considers the African diaspora north to the Middle East and the Mediterranean shore and to the west before and during the colonial period. He looks at African reaction to Western views through such movements as Pan-Africanism and Garveyism and examines contemporary Africa as a world market, as the object of international philanthropy, and as an investment platform. Concepts of alignment and nonalignment, superpower rivalry in Africa, and international forums are introduced. Black American involvement in Africa is examined through TransAfrica and the Washington Office on Africa, as well as other private and public efforts. The unit ends with an exploration of African views of the future, drawing on the Lagos Plan, the ECA study, African involvement in the NIEO, and other proposals – including the possibility of an African atomic bomb.

Primary source readings are: Marcus Garvey, "Redeeming the African Motherland"; selections from Colin Legum, *Pan-Africanism, A Short Political Guide*; and Desmond Tutu, "The Question of South Africa."

KEY WORDS AND CONCEPTS

Afro-Marxist states
Angola
apartheid
bantustans
black diaspora
Creoles
W. E. B. Du Bois
Marcus Garvey
la Route Chinoise
Organization of African Unity
Pan-African congresses
pax Pretoriana
Portuguese Revolution
TransAfrica

QUESTIONS FOR REVIEW

1. Many people still tend to think of Africa as a world apart, isolated from the mainstream of events and developments on other continents. Why does this perception persist, and why is it wrong?

2. The chapter discusses both an "internal" and an "external" African "voice." Identify each "voice" and indicate how the two merged to become one. What is the significance of each "voice" to the political development of black Africa?

3. Why has Africa become an arena for superpower rivalry? Identify several aspects of that rivalry and suggest their possible impact on African politics or economics.

4. When and why did the United States become interested in Africa? Identify the ways in which Americans became and are still involved in Africa.

5. Southern Africa, in particular the Republic of South Africa, has become the focus of intense, worldwide interest. Identify the ways in which that interest has been manifested, and suggest why Africans are often frustrated by South Africa's seeming lack of response to international pressure.

ADDITIONAL RECOMMENDED READINGS

Albright, David E. (ed.). *Africa and International Communism*. New York: Macmillan, 1980.

Bissell, Richard E. *Apartheid and International Organizations*. Boulder: Westview, 1977.

Carter, G. M., and P. O'Meara (eds.). *International Politics in Southern Africa*. Bloomington: Indiana University Press, 1982.

Cronon, David E. *Marcus Garvey*. Englewood Cliffs, N.J.: Prentice-Hall, Inc., 1973.

Du Bois, W. E. B. *The World and Africa*. New York: Viking, 1946.

Gavshon, Arthur. *Crisis in Africa: Battleground of East and West*. New York: Penguin Books, 1981.

Legum, Colin. *Pan-Africanism, A Short Political Guide*. New York: Praeger, 1962.

Le Vine, Victor T., and Timothy W. Luke. *The Arab-African Connection: Political and Economic Realities*. Boulder: Westview, 1979.

Padmore, George. *Pan-Africanism or Communism*. New York: Doubleday, 1956.

WEEK 12

Africa Is One

OBJECTIVES

After reading this week's assignments, you should be able to:

- Discuss the ways in which Egypt exemplifies the triple heritage in Africa;
- Using the Suez War and the Algerian Revolution as examples, analyze how African and Islamic political forces influenced political leaders and policies in Western Europe;
- Identify the roles of Charles de Gaulle and Harold Macmillan in decolonizing Africa.

STUDY RESOURCES

Check with your instructor for specific assignments.

Television Program
    There is no viewing assignment this week.
The Africans: A Reader
    Part III, "Africa Is One: The View from the Sahara"
    by Ali A. Mazrui
The Africans: A Triple Heritage by Ali A. Mazrui
    Chapter 14, "Between War and Peace"

STUDY FOCUS by Colin M. Turnbull

The customary Western idea that Africa can be divided neatly into North Africa and sub-Saharan Africa is a reflection of Western ignorance. For early Europeans, the northern coast was all of Africa that was really known; and that knowledge was first dominated by the obvious antiquity and greatness of Egypt, then subsequently by the rapid spread and establishment of Islam throughout the northern territory. Even when explorers and traders made contact with other coastal regions of Africa and established trading posts there, their knowledge both of those coastal cultures and of the vast interior was so superficial that the intricate relationship between southern and northern Africa escaped their detection. For example, it was long believed by Europeans that the Sahara desert was an impenetrable barrier between north and south; whereas in fact that region had not always been a desert. Even at its worst it had never prevented regular trans-Saharan trade caravans from plying back and forth, carrying with them not only goods but also ideas, customs, and religious beliefs and practices. The Europeans' unawareness of north-south relations was encouraged by a certain ethnocentrism, as well, which allows Westerners to accept the grandeur of Egypt and the racial and religious proximity of the Arab Muslims more readily than the seemingly more alien "primitive" cultures of "Black Africa."

In this chapter, Professor Mazrui sets out to dispel the Westerners' illusions and to show that "Africa is one." Rather than give a detailed history of the rich and ancient interchange between all parts of Africa, he chooses to focus principally on the contemporary scene – especially on two key events in twentieth-century African history: the Algerian Revolution of 1954-62, and the Suez War of 1956. This puts our study of Africa in a very broad perspective. Not only does he show how events in one part of Africa can influence events in the entire continent, Professor Mazrui also shows how African events can transform Europe as well as how European events can influence Africa. He explains that these two wars in northern Africa influenced the destinies of Charles de Gaulle in France and Harold Macmillan in Great Britain, the two national leaders who in turn would preside over the decolonization of Africa as a whole.

We also see in this chapter how the colonial presence, in the form of established "white settlers" – living representatives of the Western part of the triple heritage – became a factor comparable to the Islamic presence, which had long established itself throughout the continent. The personal and national pride and prestige of these immigrants influenced events as much as any rational policy. In the north, it would prolong the Algerian War long after France had released its other African colonies, and nearly lead to a military coup in France itself. And in the south it would lead South Africa to ignore Macmillan's advice to modify its internal racialist policies, instead taking the momentous step of withdrawing from the Commonwealth.

One of the many subtle factors exposed by Professor Mazrui is one that has surely left its mark in many an independent African nation: the way in which colonial powers, compelled by a coalition of indigenous and Islamic forces in Africa to "facilitate" liberation, cleverly "used the idiom of imperial grandeur in the process of making concessions to African nationalistic demands." The very process of granting freedom became a display of imperial might, of imperial mentality, and a final and enduring assertion of imperial cultural values. The Western part of the triple heritage, in the very act of apparent withdrawal, may have established itself more firmly than ever. As Mazrui demonstrates, however, the Islamic factor was a powerful counterforce to colonialist policies. And as we have seen in previous chapters, indigenous Africa was by no means passively accepting of the colonial legacy; it had its own strategies and its own ways of asserting its strength as an equal partner in the triple heritage.

STUDY FOCUS QUESTIONS

As you complete this week's assignments, consider the following questions.

- What are the ties that bind northern and sub-Saharan Africa to each other? Include political, religious, geographic, economic, social, and historical factors.
- Why did the decolonization of Africa take place when it did?
- What are some major ways that events in Africa have influenced the internal and foreign policies of France, England, and the United States?
- What is the meaning of nonalignment as it relates to African and other nations? What are its advantages and disadvantages?

KEY CONCEPTS AND NAMES

Algerian Revolution
Aswan Dam
colonialism by consent
Charles de Gaulle
Harold Macmillan
Mau Mau war
Gamal Abdel Nasser

NATO
Kwame Nkrumah
nonalignment
Suez War
Sékou Touré
World Bank

REVIEW QUESTIONS

1. Discuss the causes of the Algerian Revolution.
2. How did the Algerian Revolution affect the internal and external policies of France?
3. How did France and England fulfill their national self-interest while granting independence to their colonies in Africa?
4. What events led up to the Suez War, and how was it ended?
5. Discuss Harold Macmillan's role in the decolonization of Africa. How did he go against the position of the Tory party in this – and why?
6. What have been the steps by which white dominion of Africa abated? What do you predict for South Africa in this respect, and why?

ADDITIONAL RECOMMENDED READINGS

Kirkwood, Kenneth. *Britain in Africa*. London: Chatto and Windus, 1965.

Legum, Colin. *Africa: A Handbook*. London: Anthony Blond, 1961.

Nkrumah, Kwame. *Hands Off Africa!!!* Accra: Ministry of Local Government, 1960.

Sampson, Anthony. *Macmillan: A Study in Ambiguity*. Harmondsworth, Middlesex: Penguin Books, 1977.

United Nations. *General Assembly, 15th Session, Official Records, 896th Plenary Meeting, Friday 23rd September, 1960*. New York: United Nations, 1960.

WEEK 13

The Cultural Diaspora

OBJECTIVES

After reading this week's assignments, you should be able to:

- Briefly explain the concept of diaspora and its application to peoples of African descent, and describe the current geographic spread of the African diaspora;
- Cite examples from the disciplines of music, religion, art, and folklore of African cultural continuities, adaptations, and changes in the United States, the Caribbean, and Latin America;
- Define *Négritude* and examine the African experience and impact in Europe in art and literature;
- Discuss the influence of the diaspora on Africa, citing specific examples in music and intellectual thought.

STUDY RESOURCES

Check with your instructor for specific assignments.

Television Program
There is no viewing assignment this week.
The Africans: A Reader
Part IV, "The Cultural Diaspora"
by Mbye Cham
The Africans: A Triple Heritage by Ali A. Mazrui
"Muntu: A Conclusion"

STUDY FOCUS by Colin M. Turnbull

At the outset of our effort to come to a better, richer understanding of contemporary Africa, we took a long look at African aesthetics. At that time, we learned that an indigenous cultural foundation underlies all of life in Africa itself, and that this culture has also assimilated and adapted the Islamic and Western elements of Africa's triple heritage. In large measure the chapters that followed examined political and economic issues. We have seen that Africa's internal politics and economics have international implications in the present as in the past. Now it is right that we should turn again to a consideration of the African cultural legacy, and to a recognition that the indigenous tradition, along with the Islamic and Western parts of the triple heritage, has made itself felt throughout the world, and continues to do so. This again makes it clear that Africa is far from being isolated; it is not even remote, for it is manifest, in part, wherever people who left Africa carried their African heritage. It is claimed that even among those who deny such Africanity it is still a force; and as we saw in previous chapters it is demonstrably an increasingly powerful political, economic, and personal force among those who do recognize it.

In the final chapter of our reader, Professor Cham shows that the existence of an African diaspora actually antedates the slave trade, although slavery was the major factor in its spread. Even where relocation of Africans was involuntary, as with enslavement – and perhaps in part *because* of the highly oppressive nature of slavery in the Americas – much of the African tradition was kept alive and implanted on foreign soil. Among the clearest examples of continuity are the Yoruba beliefs and religious practices to be found in the Caribbean and South and North America, the clearly Akan culture still flourishing in the interior of Suriname, and the practice of Islam found in Georgia and the Carolina seacoast.

Just as it is often difficult if not impossible to determine "origins" of cultural practices within Africa, however, it is equally difficult – and perhaps equally unprofitable – to separate continuity from independent development with respect to the diaspora. While it is possible to point to a few clearly identifiable "pure" African elements in Afro-American culture, these can in no way fully account for the pervasive sense of Africanity to be found throughout the diaspora – for example, the indefinable African "something" that characterizes black American Christian churches, where the line that separates religion and artistic expression is very thin. Here we examine the possibilities of not only continuity of indigenous cultural elements but also an ongoing process of *adaptation*, which in itself might be said to be a cultural trait the African immigrants brought with them. The term *transformation* is also used here, and it is well worth considering adaptation and transformation as two distinct processes at work in creating what in effect might be thought of as *the multiple heritage* of the diaspora.

In this chapter, Professor Cham examines music, oral narrative, poetry, and other art forms practiced in the diaspora, all of which serve to illustrate Africanity, or "Négritude." The reader who wants to penetrate that mystery will be challenged to go beyond technical analysis, for the essential Africanity of these religious and art forms does not lie in the specifics of rhythm or melody or meter – least of all when we analyze African art (or religion) in terms of Western aesthetics or religious concepts. The existence of so many magnificent examples of African art in our museums and private collections makes analysis of form all too easy. But those museums and collections can never provide the context; and without that, some say, the pieces are no longer African in any but an empty, mechanical sense. What Western artists find in African art says more about themselves, about *their* skill at adaptation and transformation, than it does about Africa. The essential Africanity lies less in form than in spirit – or, soul.

In some of the readings with which Professor Cham's chapter ends, we see something of the conflict felt by individuals who have had to face the pull of various cultures in their own lifetimes, living for years in the West, then going back to Africa with a changed vision of Africa, only to find that that too has changed. We are also given examples of how differently various members of the diaspora have reacted to a "return to Africa," deriving from such a return (physical, intellectual, emotional) such varied emotions as hope, despair, comfort, and grief.

The essence of Africanity is probably stated as clearly as it can be toward the end of the excerpt from Abioseh Nicol's "The Meaning of Africa." There he says of his eventual return to his homeland and of his rediscovery of what it is to be African:

> You are not a country, Africa,
> You are a concept . . .

and:

> I know now that is what you are, Africa:
> Happiness, contentment, and fulfillment,
> And a small bird singing in a mango tree.

This is the kind of thinking, with *feeling*, that we are encouraged to bring to our study of the diaspora, not only in terms of what it has brought from Africa and given to the rest of the world, but in terms of what it has given back to Africa.

Primary source readings for the text chapter include selections from the following: Alain Locke, *Negro Art: Past and Present*; Jacques Louis Hymans, *Léopold Sédar Senghor: An Intellectual Biography*; Francis Ernest Kobina Parkes, "Ghana"; Gabriel Okara, ". . . And the Other Immigrant"; Jacques Roumain, "Guinea"; and Abioseh Nicol, "The Meaning of Africa."

STUDY FOCUS QUESTIONS

As you complete this week's assignments, consider the following questions.

- How was the African diaspora created?
- What African cultural elements have been retained by communities in the diaspora?
- Give examples of ways that the triple heritage has been expanded in the diaspora to become the multiple heritage.
- How has the diaspora culture influenced Africa itself?

KEY CONCEPTS AND NAMES

abstraction
avant-garde
blues
cultural hegemony
diaspora
dualism
ethnographic museums
ethos
Harlem Renaissance
Négritude
oral narrative
rap music
Léopold Sédar Senghor
symbolism
trickster narratives

REVIEW QUESTIONS

1. Discuss Léopold Sédar Senghor's biography and his concept of Négritude.

2. What is the history of African art's influence on the West? How do you see the future of the influence of African art?

3. What black cultural movements besides Négritude have emerged from the diaspora, and what were their goals? How has Africa been important in these renaissances of black culture?

4. Looking back into previous chapters, as well as this chapter, explain as fully as possible Alioune Diop's statement that Afro-Americans spoke for Africans when they could not speak for themselves.

5. Name as many activities as you can that belong to the Afro-American cultural tradition, including the arts, the crafts, and verbal and musical expression. Which of these activities are generally included among the "fine arts" in the West? Devise an argument for expanding the definition of fine arts to include more of the Afro-American heritage.

ADDITIONAL RECOMMENDED READINGS

Courlander, Harold. *A Treasury of Afro-American Folklore.* New York: Crown Publishers, 1976.

do Nascimiento, Abdias. "Quilombismo and the Afro-Brazilian Artist." *Caribe* (April 1980): 16-17.

Herskovits, Melville. *The Myth of the Negro Past.* New York: Harper and Brothers, 1941.

Hymans, Jacques. *Léopold Sédar Senghor: An Intellectual Biography.* Edinburgh: University of Edinburgh Press, 1971.

Jones, Leroi (Amiri Baraka). *Blues People . . . Negro Music in White America.* New York: William Morrow and Co., 1963.

Kennedy, Ellen C. (ed.). *The Négritude Poets.* New York: Viking, 1975.

Locke, Alain. *Negro Art: Past and Present.* Washington, D.C.: Associates in Negro Folk Education, 1936.

Mark, Peter A. "African Influences in Contemporary Black American Painting." *Art Voices* (Jan.-Feb. 1981): 15-19.

Ramos, Arthur. *The Negro in Brazil.* Washington, D.C.: Associated Publishers, Inc., 1939.

Smart, Ian. *Central American Writers of Caribbean Origin: A New Hispanic Literature*. Washington, D.C.: Three Continents Press, 1984.

Snowden, Frank. *Blacks in Antiquity: Ethiopians in the Greco-Roman Experience*. Cambridge: Harvard University Press, 1970.

Southern, Eileen. *Music of Black Americans*. New York: Norton, 1983.

Van Sertima, Ivan. *They Came Before Columbus*. New York: Random House, 1976.

Warner, Keith Q. *Kaiso! The Calypso as Oral Literature*. Washington, D.C.: Three Continents Press, 1982.